I0119124

POETRY OF A LIFE INTERRUPTED

Caroline Clancy

chipmunkapublishing
the mental health publisher

Caroline Clancy

Published by
Chipmunkapublishing
United Kingdom

http://www.chipmunkapublishing.com

ISBN   978-1-78382-429-8

TO ALL THE WARRIOR WOMEN OF THE WORLD WHO REFUSED TO GIVE UP, WHO FOUGHT, RECOVERED, AND ARE NOW SURVIVORS.

Caroline Clancy

Anger will eat you alive,
Turn you inside out.
Cause any number of physical complaints,
Use overwhelming amounts of,
Physical and emotional energy.
Beware the anger that twists your insides,
Spreading venom and bitterness,
Through body, mind and soul.
Anger cripples our ability to think,
Too function within blame, and hatred.
Release it and then let it go,
Before it grows into a huge chip on your,
Shoulders.
Before it weighs you down, burdens you,
Destroying any last fragments,
Of peace of mind, let it go.
For it has the power to destroy you,
Your mind, your soul,
Your Life.

1

---

[1] This piece of poetry is about the strong feelings of anger. All my life anger has frightened me, particularly uncontrollable anger.

We are not born to be alone,
We are social beings.
Yet there is so much loneliness,
In this World it's heartbreaking.
Our Technological society,
Has pulled us all into our homes,
And we forget about,
All the lonely people beyond,
Our own front doors. [2]

---

[2] I believe that technology, computers, mobile phones and gaming have made us less social beings. We spend too much time using technology and not enough time on face to face conversations. This generates feelings of isolation.

Sometimes I felt lost at Sea, [3]
Within me my thoughts and feelings,
Seemed senseless to me.
There appeared to be no starting point,
For sorting out the mess within.
Neither was there a finishing point,
Because life continues way after,
The mess I was lost in had made some sense.
Lost at a Sea with no anchors,
I felt like the Ancient Mariners,
Although I seemed to be seasick,
Tossed on the waves of feelings,
Then crashing onto the shore, the rocks,
The pebbles and the sand.
Eventually the Sea spat me out renewed,
Reenergised and mostly recovered.
And I wasn't so lost anymore after all.

---

[3] The feeling in life of being lost. Having no sense of direction
before finding the will to work towards Recovery.

The love my Father showed me,
Wasn't love at all.
It was a violation of my trust,
Abuse of any kind is not love.
Instead it's sickening traumatic experiences,
Which can n no way be called love.
Not in any true sense of the word.
Love, real love, is kindness,
With compassion and empathy,
Understanding, caring, patience.
Real love shouldn't hurt at all.

There were no boundaries,
Between my Father and I.
No physical boundaries,
Sexual boundaries.
The only boundaries that,
Truly existed were those of,
The alpha male versus the tiny child.[4]
Authoritarian and controlling,
Disciplinarian and rule maker,
Punisher of wrongdoings.
Mockery and sarcasm,
Reducing me too tears.
No reason to consider,
A tiny child's feelings,
For the adult parent ruled.
No room for consideration,
Understanding,
Love or empathy.
For these boundaries were,
Made crystal clear,
Relentlessly.

---

[4] Without boundaries it is difficult for children to grow into separate individuals with their own self-identity.

Overthinking overwhelming unquiet Mind,
Imploding, exploding, nuclear reaction,
Thoughts flying through the night sky,
Faster than a comet, in a blink of an eye.
Not that I ever wanted, a Mind,
Like the overworked one I have.
Too fast, far too fast, never any signs of slowing.
Slowing enough to process,
Just one thought fully that my Mind,
Is an exhausting overthinking Bipolar Mind.
Overwhelming thoughts at the speed of light.
No respite from the torrential thoughts,
No respect for a body that requires rest.
Overthinking overwhelming unquiet Mind,
Driving me insane with its incessant,
White noise, a killer in my head, uninvited,
Inextricably linked to every [5]fibre of my body.

---

[5] I find it very difficult being bipolar. It's called the "unquiet mind", a description that is certainly true. My mind thinks at a fast rate of knots. My thoughts tumble over each other and never stop. I do not know what it is to have a silent calm mind. It can feel exceedingly overwhelming.

It's okay not to be okay, [6]
Despite what others might,
Think or say.
No one would choose,
To suffer so,
With any mental illness.
It's okay not to be okay,
As long as you,
Seek and find,
Both the help and support,
That you deserve and need.
Ignore the ignorant,
Who turn away.
Those weren't real friends,
Ignorance isn't an excuse,
For rudeness and mockery.
No one would choose,
To suffer so much.
It's okay not to be okay,
Seek the help,
You deserve.

---

[6] Mental illnesses shouldn't be shamed. Just because it's an invisible illness doesn't mean that it doesn't hurt. Mental health issues are as valid as physical health issues.

My Father was the Joker,
A master of mockery and sarcasm.
Belittling and bullying.
There was nothing humorous,
About my Fathers scathing jokes.
My Father though found his jokes,
Hysterically funny, so, so, funny.
Laughing at my feelings, my words,
My fears and my clumsiness.
Laughing at his own jokes,
Until I'd be reduced to tears.
Then my Father would get angry.
Angry that I couldn't take a joke.
Tears were for babies,
Turn off the bloody taps, he'd snap.
As if it were that simple,
To stop crying just like that.
My feelings were shamed,
Never validated in any way.
The master Joker wasn't bothered,
It was almost as if he enjoyed,
Provoking such a strong reaction.
I couldn't help crying,
I hadn't learned self control,
I was only five years old.

My Father said he loved me, his daughter,
But it wasn't love that he showed me.
Sexual abuse isn't love, it's the opposite.
Like the ashes of burnt red roses, meaningless.
The word 'love' is to freely used,
It's used so often it becomes a meaningless
word.
Physical, mental and emotional abuse,
Are not love, quite the reverse.
Saying that you 'love ' someone,
Doesn't always make it true.
Love is a feeling engendered on compassion,
Understanding, empathy and caring, not abuse.
My Fathers love was like the ashes,
Of the burning roses,
Destroyed by himself, for reasons only,
He would know, or could have answered.
Love is the unconditional infinite,
Truth of feeling, the Love I have,
For my own two children. [7]

---

[7] A fathers love for his daughter should not be such that he
mentally, physically , emotionally destroys his child. A parent that
abuses his child, is not a loving parent.

Childhood demons,
Choking, suffocating,
The life slowly from,
My lungs.
Gagging and gasping,
For life given oxygen,
Head swimming,
Jaw clamped open .
As Darkness took control,
Stealing my innocence,
Under the blanket of the,
Darkest nights.
Lungs straining,
Heart beat pounding,
Thumping in my ears.
Held captive, unable,
To seek release,
From the death,
Creeping through my body,
Towards my exploding,
Heart. [8]

---

[8] The sexual abuse I suffered traumatised me. I did not understand for years that oral sex was classed as abuse. I believed that only rape was classed as sexual abuse.

It's a bizarre strange feeling to feel,
Nothing, no personality, no self-identity.
Just nothing, nothing worthwhile at all.
Emotionally empty, to the point where,
I valued nothing about myself at all.
All I knew was that if pushed between,
A rock and a hard place, I'd say,
Without a doubt that I was utterly disgusting,
A nobody, hardly human at all.
Reflections in a mirror meant nothing,
I failed to see myself as others did.
I saw myself instead as a shameful,
Example of how a woman shouldn't be.
I saw in the mirror 'Nothing',
Nothing at all, my identity.
I hated every single part of myself,
From top to toe and inside out.
When asked how I felt I never said,
I said instead, 'I'm fine ',[9]
Which meant precisely 'nothing' at all,
A bizarre answer to the question,
Which was met with ignorant silence.
Thus proving me right each and every time,
That Nothing was indeed, exactly what I was.

---

[9] The diagnosis of Bipolar 2 disorder isn't an easy condition to live with. Recovery meant applying what I had learned at University (ethics and philosophy) and using those skills to think differently.

I Recovered because the small flicker of hope,
That I barely recognised as a child,
After years of lying almost dormant,
Flared up when I realised that my future,
Was in my hands and mine alone.
Discovering that I was the only one that could,
Save myself, that no other person could,
I suddenly became aware of all those,
Long and wasted years,
Spent expecting others to save me instead.
My mindset being Bipolar,
Had always been rigid black and white.
Overwhelming overthinking,
So I changed this with logic,
Adjusting my mindset accordingly so.
To begin with it was difficult,
But became easier over time.
Good results spurred me on further,
As the light of hope within me, flared brightly,
In response to these efforts that I made.
Recovery is living in the Present,
Whilst acknowledging the Past,
But concentrating on the moment,
And letting go of the Past.

I was my Fathers puppet on a string,
In the end he'd only have to yank one string,
Hard occasionally to remind me of my place.
And obedience was my name,
From childhood to adulthood I was submissive,
To the point where just a lot from my Father,
Would leave me shaking in my shoes.
There wasn't any choice about anything at all,
He got exactly what he wanted through,
Authoritarian rule and control.
I used to wonder, had I been different,
Perhaps I'd not have ended up,
My Fathers puppet on a string.
But truth is that it started when I was,
So very young and small,
I was without a doubt my Fathers,
Brainwashed puppet on a string. [10]

---

[10] My Father was authoritarian and as a child I felt completely controlled by him. I cannot possibly imagine how I could have reacted any differently to such a commanding and authoritative man as my father.

Caroline Clancy

Follow your heart?
I dragged mine,
Behind me,
Treated it badly,
Cause that's what,
My Father did.
I thought he,
Knew best.
Stupid childish,
Heart.
Never deserving,
Any love.
So I dragged,
My heart,
Behind me,
No more than,
It deserved.
Through,
Dirty muddy puddles,
And shitty,
Pavements.
Exactly what,
My heart deserved.
So I dragged,
My heart, my heavy burden,
Behind me always.

Anxiety crushes my mind and soul,
Squeezing my wind pipe hard,
Whilst my mind floats due to lack of oxygen,
Making me gasp, hyperventilate.
Too many thoughts and worries rushing,
Like a tornado through my mind.
Perspiration forming on my brow,
Palms cold and clammy, pale in colour,
Anxiety feeling like a rollercoaster.
I wast it to stop, but it's not listening.
Breathe, I think, breathe!
I try hard to take some control,
But unfortunately I've started too late.
Then the tears come, steaming, cascading,
A torrential downpour.
As they slowly subside and breathing,
Becomes easier, exhaustion takes over,
From the finally diminishing,
Anxiety attack, and I become calmer. [11]

---

[11] *Anxiety attacks that become panic attacks are without a doubt some of the Morse symptoms of mental illnesses. I've actually been admitted to hospital after a terrible panic attack felt like a heart attack.*

Smothered, suffocating, smell,
Pouring into my nostrils.
Mouth full and tight,
Jaw cracking resounding,
Reverberating inside my ears.
I hear too my own blood pumping.
Heart beat accelerating,
My head feels as if it's,
About to burst wide open,
Blood splattering Darkness,
As I died.
Snot and tears not helping,
Suffocating,
Sparky dots behind my eyes.
Chest heaving, gasping,
Thundering pulse on my ear drums,
Like a thousand horses running,
Fading, fading, fading…..
And then it stops.
I fall back onto my bed covers,
Hearing Darkness leaving.
Left crying and dragging in air,
Wiping snot on my cotton nightdress,
Spitting, coughing, spitting.
Silence and exhaustion,
Leaving me blankly staring at nothing,
Nothing at all.[12]

---

[12] Oral sexual abuse, this is when I began dissociating.

My Father knew what he was doing, [13]
He must have understood his wrongdoing,
For he isolated me, in the family,
From making friends, or going to parties.
Isolation is the key to silencing a child.
It worked particularly well with me,
Ensuring I was submissive, compliant,
Well behaved, quiet and disciplined.
Afraid of his authority and absolute control,
He needn't have asked me to keep secrets,
For I'd never have dared to tell.
The tone of his voice, the look in his eyes,
We're more than enough to ensure,
That I never ever spoke,
Of life behind our closed front door.
Isolation worked well for my Father,
A terrified child isolated n misery,
Not understanding but knowing not to ask.
Just one look from my Father,
And I'd be cowering in a corner.
There really hadn't been any need to,
Spell silence and secret out for me.
I just knew silence was necessary.

---

[13] My Father was an exceedingly powerful influence in my life. He
was able to silence me with a look or his tone of voice.

Silence can be violent, as can a facial expression,
The violence wasn't only sexual and physical.
Most of the violence was mental and emotional,
My Fathers words were harsh,
Impatient with my slowness,
Annoyance at my imperfections,
Disgust at my stupidity.
His words tore through me like a whip lash,
His irritation at my tears, my fears, myself,
Ensured that I had no self confidence,
No self esteem, no sense of worthiness.
His mockery and sarcasm shamed me.
His silence terrified me for it ensured imminent,
Punishment, though I never remembered why.
Mental and emotional violence are as distressing
In a different way to physical and sexual abuse.
But the trauma can be just as high,
Lasting longer, until his death and beyond.
There is violence in a silence that screams,
White noise and the brainwashing,
Of a child to an adult.
Words last far longer in ones thoughts,
Whoever said words don't hurt, Lied.[14]

---

[14] Most of the mental abuse from my Father was in the form of mockery and sarcasm. He reduced me to tears by making unkind jokes about me, and then became irritated and angry that I was upset. This continually undermined my feelings and invalidated them continually.

I am invisible, you cannot see I, [15]
For I has an identity,
So I'm not an I you see.
Instead the invisible child,
Lost teenager,
Broken adult.
That's the I if me.
I am invisible, you cannot hear I,
I had no voice,
Not heard,
Voiceless and invalidated,
That's the I of me.
I am invisible, you cannot touch me,
My body will hurt you,
Like touch hurts me, you see.
I am invisible,
I am not an I,
But a me.
Me is nothing,
Empty, broken , shattered,
Unidentifiable.
That's me.

---

[15] I actually believed that I was invisible during periods of my childhood.

Behind the closed doors of our family home,
Authoritarian control, ruled ruthlessly.
Anyone passing our house would never know,
That within its walls lived an abused child.
Had they known, would they have cared?
In a society that prefers to turn the other way,
To not see the truth, not get involved,
An attitude of its none of my business,
I've got better things to do.
Thus to turn a blind eye, to not get involved.
Where are the good Samaritans,
When you need them?
Hiding in their homes behind twitchy curtains,
Curiosity killed the cat,
Their think g to themselves
And they may well have been right. [16]

---

[16] It's amazing how during the 1960s that abuse awareness was so low. There were far fewer Social workers and childline

Unaware of my childhood traumatic amnesia,
The years that followed were lived in,
Utter confusion, a total inability to,
Bridge the gap between childhood and older.
Unable to understand the reasons,
As to why I was like I was.
Not understanding why I as such an outcast,
So unable to fit into my surroundings.
I instinctively knew that I was different,
By the way others reacted to me.
As the years passed,
The gap between myself and others,
Widened with every passing year.
I couldn't relate to my peers,
Any adults or my teachers so that by the time,
I reached University the self-harming,
Had already begun.
It felt as if I were drowning under water,
Whilst all others were able to swim.
The confusion inside me rolled like fog,
Through my mind disabling me.
Keeping my smiling mask in place,
Became so much harder.
These were the isolated lost years,
For which I had no,
Understanding or insight,
Couldn't reason or explain why I was like this,
Not even too myself.

My Father who declared himself a perfectionist,
Wanted a carbon copy of himself in me.
Two first class honours degrees from University.
My Father had exceedingly high expectations,
Of me in absolutely everything.
I failed miserably to match his standards,
In every way possible as a young child.
Nothing I ever produced at school was ever,
Good enough for my Father.
Criticism was my Fathers middle name.
By eight years or age, I believed myself a failure,
My Father didn't disagree with me.
Stupidity irritated him more than anything,
The more pressure he applied,
The more I failed and cried.
Strangely years later I achieved,
A first class degree from University.
But to my horror I overheard my Father,
Belittle my degree to my brother.
Mine was an Arts degree,
Whilst my brothers was a Science degree.
Obviously the better one, since it was scientific.
That was the day I finally realised,
That nothing I ever did, would ever please him,
And from that day forth I gave up trying,
To please a man who could clearly never,
Be pleased by me.

Damaged, broken, shattered,
Accurately describes the feelings I felt.
Nothing resembling a 'normal ' person.
For the damage runs deep,
Deep inside the body, soul and mind.
Embedded into my bone marrow
Running though my veins,
Beating through my heart,
Engulfing my brain.
That's the depth of the damage,
I felt.
The damage I had to,
Face and gouge out,
In order to,
Recover,
Enough to live,
My Life.

I couldn't have imagined the Asylum before, [17]
Not in my wildest dreams or nightmares.
I knew nothing of psychiatric Institutions,
Neither mental health issues or medications.
Knew nothing about psychiatry or Psychiatrists.
So admission to the Asylum was shocking,
Its old decaying building, locked doors,
Barred windows, dirty carpets, cracked linoleum,
Handprints on pale green institutional walls,
Mixed wards with little or no privacy.
Continual noise in an environment of unleashed,
Distress, weeping, screaming, shouting and,
Sometimes violence.
The environment where expectations of
recovery,
Almost nonexistent, unexpected,
Rarely discussed in any meaningful way,
Where the revolving door syndrome was high,
For those that unlike I had a,
Consultant Psychiatrist who was able to reason.
Chances of getting out were nonexistent,
For myself and the five other female patients,
That our Consultant kept under lock and key,
For the entire decade that followed.

---

[17] The Asylum was in South London, built in 1886. It was as described. After ten years in the Asylum we were all moved out due to Health and Safety reasons. A couple of months later the building was demolished and modern flats built where it had once stood.

In his own way my Father made me a prisoner,
Of his own mind and behaviours,
As if I were shackled to him from birth.
Lack of boundaries made this feeling worse,
Not knowing where he finished and I started.
His abuse made me his prisoner through,
His own secrets and lies.

The way he spoke to me imprisoned,
My own speech in utter silence.
I might as well have been locked in his mind,
For his disciplinarian rules kept a tight rein.
I couldn't be anything other than he wanted,
For fear of punishment, for usurping his rules.
As a prisoner of my Fathers mind,
I was only ever required to demonstrate,
Obedience, submissiveness and silence,
Absolutely nothing more,
Than exactly what my Father expected,
Or face the consequences.

Through the mirror cracked,
My image wildly distorted.
Matching the brokenness,
Within and all imperfections.
The secrets that were once,
Hidden deep inside my soul,
Now we're visible to the world.
My shame is inextricably,
Interwoven with my Past.
Seemingly everlasting,
Constant reminders of ,
The abuses of the flesh,
The violations.
And the resulting,
Self-punishments,
Now feint scars so pale. [18]

---

[18] It is impossible to have a good self image after years of abuse. I saw myself as some abnormal being, and used self-harm to punish myself for never being good enough to be loved.

Illnesses of the mind are of the most,
Complex kind.
For they are individual illnesses,
Unique to every sufferer.
Making symptoms, treatments and medications,
Differing according to every individual.
Our mental health services fail because of this,
Failing to see each of us as individuals.
But rather herded like animals,
As groups under different labels.
We need a more holistic approach,
One hat treats individuals as individuals,
In body, mind and soul.
A whole new philosophy of,
Mental health care, one that turns,
Around the exponential growth,
With each and every passing year,
The huge number of cases of mental illnesses,
Which are still relentlessly growing.
Resulting in suffering, more suffering,
Demonstrating the certain need for Change. [19]

---

[19] Over the last thirty years I have become more and more convinced that a more holistic approach to mental health care is needed. I still see it as the revolving -door system. You become an inpatient after a crisis and when you return to the community there is insufficient help, and a crises reoccurs.

Black roses for death,
Black for Darkness,
Lying in the casket,
Oblivious to the congregation,
Obliged to be seated,
To listen to the requiem,
Vivaldi's Spring,
Despite it being Autumn,
The crisp brown leaves,
Crackling under feet.
Knowing that I feel nothing,
Sitting in that silence.
Hearing words that,
Seem meaningless.
I do not feel anything,
Except for relief,
That he's gone,
And the guilt I,
Associated with that.

Emotional abuse is demeaning,
Mockery and sarcasm humiliating,
Taunts stealing self-confidence,
Jibes tearing away at my self-esteem.
Inappropriate personal remarks,
Shaming and destructive.
Terrifying threats,
Breeding insecurities.
Fear of abandonment,
Secrets and lies,
Loyalty testing,
Confidence breaking.
Blaming causing guilty feelings.
Bargaining creating fear,
Bribery causing awkwardness.
Emotional abuse stripping,
Layer after layer of,
Self-esteem and confidence,
Leaving nothing but,
A messed-up,
Emotional wreck,
That has since played havoc,
My entire life through.

Growing up loathing my own body,
Disgusted with it and by it.
Ashamed of my nakedness,
Refusing to look at my reflection,
Abhorring my own body.
Hating puberty it's natural progression.
My Father celebrating my first period,
Telling my grandmother in public.
Than stating moments later,
'I wish she could stay my little girl forever '.
Despising my body more and more,
With every single passing year.
My Fathers personal comments,
Upsetting me ceaselessly.
'How's my busty blonde', at the supper table.
'Come here wench' and, [20]
'Don't dress like a whore',
'Make-up is slutty, wash your face,'
'For Gods sake high heels are for prostitutes'.
'You're not going anywhere in those my girl',
'Is that what you want men to believe'.
By the time I was sixteen, my hatred,
Towards my own body was venomous.
I loathed myself, completely. [21]

---

[20] My Fathers view of my sexuality was exceedingly disrespectful and distressing. I could not understand his attitude towards my body, clothes, teenage years. My body image reached an all time low.

[21] Physical abuse terrified me. My Father could make me wait up to forty minutes before coming up the stairs. By the time he'd arrive I was already so petrified I'd dissociated. The fact that he then stripped me of my clothes, put me across his knees and smacked me was something I 'watched' from above. I was never clear why I needed to be stripped in order to be smacked.

As a child the fear of physical punishment,
Was more terrifying than the abuse itself.
The waiting at my bedroom door for my Fathers,
Footsteps as he climbed the stairs,
For the forty minutes he'd kept me waiting,
Those were the fear inducing minutes.
Minutes filled with terror and expectation.
For each and every single minute,
Felt as long as one hour.
A reflection of how terrifying I found my Father.
By the time I'd hear him mounting the stairs,
I'd have already dissociated through utter fear.
That's how much my own Father,
Terrified my body, soul and mind.

Silence the Child, [22]
The Teenager too,
Silence the mentally ill,
Adult with medications,
To silence her will.

---

[22] Silence surrounding sexual abuse and mental illnesses is still a significant problem. In the 1970-1990s it was far worse. But there is still a lot of work that needs to be done to significantly reduce the stigma that still exists today.

Bipolar,
Black and White,
Thinking,
Overwhelming,
Overthinking.
A million shades of,
Grey between.
Black and White,
Thinking,
Exhausting,
Re-thinking,
New mindset,
To compensate,
Open the mind,
To different,
Thinking.
More,
Overwhelming, [23]
Overthinking,
Is the,
Resounding,
Result,
Of being bipolar.
Enough.

---

[23] Personally I hate being bipolar and cannot understand those that seem to revel in the disorder. My mania is rarely high, and my depression too low.

Somewhere in time,
Is the person I might have been.
If at each crossroads,
I'd chosen a different direction.
I might have gone a whole,
Multitude of other ways,
If every decision I'd made,
Had been a different one.
Then maybe there is another me,
Lost somewhere in time,
Whose life is a more stable one?
If nothing else it's a different,
Way of seeing, a different perspective,
On how my life might have been.
The idea that every choice we make,
Effects the outcome of our lives. [24]

---

[24] It's always fascinated me, the idea that a persons choices can make such a difference to their lives. Unfortunately my choices were taken away from me at an age where I had no idea what was happening. The result of this is that every choice after this was based on poor understanding and judgement.

What do you do when your whole Life,
Changes in the blink of an eye.
In one single day,
I was admitted to the Asylum, [25]
And at the very same time,
Abandoned by my entire family.
What do you do when your home is an Asylum,
And the white noise inside my head explodes.
Where the building is decaying, dank and dirty.
With mixed sex wards,
With only curtains separating each bed.
An environment so utterly chaotic,
That it's quite impossible to think.
What do you do when everything and everyone,
You knew disappears overnight.
Where suddenly nothing at all is familiar,
The underlying violence of the environment,
Frightening and overwhelming.
Where every single person is a stranger,
All that I can remember is sitting alone,
On my bed crying,
Terrified of my surroundings,
And the idea that I must be,
Utterly insane to be there.

---

[25] The fact that I'd come from a conservative middle class home
into the Asylum was a huge shock to me system. The fact that I
was then abandoned by every family member is something I've
never completely recovered from. It certainly made it far more
difficult to leave the Asylum.

Bipolar confusion due to overwhelming,
Overthinking causing misunderstandings.
It's utterly frustrating when speaking,
To have the relentless overthinking,
White noise inside my head,
At the same time as trying to listen,
To concentrate, to speak, to be heard.
My words when I finally am able to concentrate,
Often come out sounding aggressive.
Aggression has absolutely nothing to do with it,
Frustration meanwhile is the true answer.
It's difficult sometimes to hold a conversation,
Whilst inside, my mind is overthinking,
Absolutely everything.
So whilst my words might sound aggressive,
In truth I am merely frustrated.
Too much noise inside my head,
Mixing and muddling with the outside noise.
It's like having an internal radio,
Static sounding aggressive.
My bipolar disorder,
Is my greatest frustration.
Bipolar conversations can be,
An utter nightmare.
Bipolar disorder is completely exhausting.

End the Silence surrounding the Stigma,
Of mental illnesses.
Were no longer living in the dark ages!
Shoutout loud to all the ignorant,
Who still believe mental illnesses are
contagious!
Raise your voice above the shamed silence.
The only shame belongs to the ignorant.
Those that turn aside and look away,
Because they're cowards who haven't suffered.
Shoutout loud, clear as a bell, pierce the air,
With the truth of mental illnesses.
The Stigma is outdated,
Unacceptable and ultimately harmful.
So end the silence, now.

I remember the abuse, the way it made me feel.
Naked and ashamed, nauseated and disgusted.
Talking about Him and what he had done,
Felt both surreal or unreal or both.
Silent so long that the words,
When they finally came,
Gagged and choked inside my throat.
Finally when I had the courage to speak,
The words crept from between my lips,
In a hoarse whisper of utter shame.
It hadn't occurred to me that one day,
I would have to speak about these terrifying,
Images inside my head.
To say that it was hard would be,
A horrendous understatement.
That I was finally heard, believed,
And validated,
Brought tears streaming down my face.
The utter relief of finally speaking those words,
A huge and heavy burden,
Finally lifted from my Soul.
Remembering the abuse and speaking of it,
Finally broke the silence of three decades,
And with it lifted my burden of guilt,
With the truth of innocence stolen. [26]

---

[26] There is never enough time to do all the things we would perhaps like to in our lives. I believe that we should be more open to those living around us in order that people do not feel rejected, lonely or outcast.

Living and dying in a World,
That so often shows no mercy,
That doesn't seem to care about our lives at all,
Too busy to slow down.
To take a minute to show concern.
Lives entangled in the human race,
Which isn't a race for we all die in the end.
So why not slow down,
Take a minute to catch your breath.
Consider priorities like family,
Those that seem unhappy.
To start a conversation that may,
Just save a life because you took the,
Time to listen and hear,
Showed compassion, empathy, kindness,
And understanding.
You may never know what your time,
Meant too another.
So slow down and look around,
We're all going to die in the end anyhow.
Use your time wisely, care more, live more,
Love more and share more of your time.
Just because, and in case,
Your time turns out sooner than you think.

Sometimes life hits you full force in the face,
Like a meteor strike,
Lifting you off the ground,
All in that moment,
Enlightenment shines through.
You suddenly realise that your life has been,
Exhaustingly complex at every single turn.
And then you wonder,
What was it all about,
This complex life of suffering.
What was it really about?

There are demons in my head,
Screaming for release.
They want me Dead.
They came with the addiction,
And withdrawals.
Screeching and wailing like banshees.
Demanding and clawing within my mind.
They want me Dead.
Out of nowhere they came,
Turning my entire life upside down. [27]
Twenty four hours a day, no relief.
Overwhelming my mind to the point of,
Distress and suicidal ideation.
There are demons inside my head,
Screaming for release.
They want me Dead.

---

[27] In November 2016 it was discovered that my previous GP had badly over prescribed my medication for over two years. I was on 20mg of Lorazepam a day/ 140mg/week 560mg a month which is over 14,000mg during that period. I have been in withdrawals ever since. The GP admitted to being at fault. After being out of Psychiatric Hospitals for almost 18 years I found myself readmitted 4 times to date, due to the terrible withdrawals.

Indistinct, indistinguishable, irritability,
Over nothing and everything.
Tears that come for the slightest reason,
Or for no reason whatsoever.
Anger that flares suddenly frustrating,
Depression that threatens suffocation.
Thoughts overwhelming.
Tears abiding everlasting.
The end is infinitely invisible.

Each day I wonder how much longer,
I can last living,
Through the ravages of withdrawals.
Collateral damage building fast,
Wearing me down.
Each and every day,
Every hour, minute, each second,
That passes I wonder,
How much longer I can hold on.
I cannot hold on forever. [28]

---

[28] It is true that after trauma there will eventually come a time where it is impossible to pretend even to oneself that you are coping. Recovery can only begin once the trauma and its effects have been dealt with.

Death returns regularly.
It's arms hold me tight.
Hands that try to suffocate me,
Death grips as tight as a vice.
Thoughts in my mind encourage,
Deaths daily visitations.
It didn't use to be like this.
Addiction withdrawals,
Are the magnet of suffering,
That draws death upon my soul.
I have no control over,
Deadly visitations that overwhelm,
My overthinking and over stressed,
Mind, body and soul.

My brain requires concoctions,
Medications that are,
Reducing relentlessly and constantly.
My mind screams in protest,
At its lack of satisfaction
Caused by withdrawals and the,
Failure to receive medication.
My mind demands satisfaction with,
Utter ferocity.
I'm helpless in this fight,
Between death and addiction,
Unable to provide my brain,
With that which it screams for.
Death visits so often,
I've forgotten what it was like before.
Before my negligent doctor,
Blew a hole straight through my brain tissue.
Thus shattering all reason,
Stealing all joy, [29]
Leaving me alone and on my knees,
Praying, begging for redemption,
For an end to this awful suffering. [30]

---

[29] Withdrawals include major depressive disorder, suicidal
thoughts, high anxiety, panic attacks, nausea, pain,
Muscle spasms, shaking, short-term memory loss, insomnia ,
nightmares, etc… none of which are pleasant

Prescribed drug addiction,
Strips layers from my mind and body.
Like peeling the layers,
One by one from an onion.
Streaming tears, the layers peel back,
Leaving the ugliness of Addiction
For all to See.
For it is ugly when you're on your,
Hands and knees searching the garbage,
For imaginary tablets I may have missed,
Whilst praying to God,
For relief from this unspeakable,
Grubbiness of addiction overpowering
All sense and reason.

Behaviours I'd never imagined possible,
Until the awfulness of withdrawals,
Kicked in hard.
The shame and fear addiction brings,
Overwhelming, overpowering, overthinking,
Suffering, suffocating my mind,
With addiction withdrawals.
And it is grubby, it is dirty, it is shaming,
Regardless of how it occurred.
For it demonstrates how low,
Ones mind is prepared to go dragging,
Ones body through it's wake,
For something, for anything, that might,
Take away the screaming,
Unfulfilled addiction withdrawals. [31]
The like of which cause bizarre habits,
Like I've never seen in myself before.
Reducing me to the lowest of the lowest.
Self-disgust tormenting my mind and soul,
Every single day that passes.

---

[31] The major depression caused by withdrawals is the worst depression I've ever experienced in my entire life.

Addiction screaming through my mind,
Roaring like a volcano alive,
A tsunami of feelings overriding reason,
A tornado force ripping apart my body.
Lightening strikes piercing my,
Overwhelming overthinking mind.
From the darkness of Addiction,
Before me lies a Desert, without an oasis.
No relief, just endless landscapes of nothing.
But the barren heat of desperation,
That results from prescribed drug addiction.
There are absolutely no,
Landscapes that relieve the,
Utter desperation that my body feels,
For the drug that is being withdrawn,
Sickening me through and through.
To the point that I'd gladly decapitate myself,
In order to feel nothing at all.
In order not to feel. The World is oblivious to
each of our struggles,
It passes us by without a sideways glance.
Ignorant of personal suffering,
Blind to the tears of anguish, the sound of pain.
Life carries on by without a thought.
Just as it always has done,
Generation after generation.
Timelessness constant in it's blindness.
I stand and stare beside my window,
At the passing people. (Cont)

Thinking, believing that my pain,
Must surely radiate, in noise, in light,
Like an aura surrounding me.
My imagination runs riotously and I wonder,
Don't these people see the ruin of me?
Then I wonder about those lives I watch,
How their lives are, do any of them feel like me?
A life ruined by medication mistakenly,
Prescribed by a negligent doctor.
Not that it makes any difference to me now,
For its far far too late to correct this mistake.
That times long passed, three years ago.
I watch the oblivious people,
Why should they care about my suffering,
The troubles of an unknown stranger.

What do you do when addiction takes hold,
Outside, inside, within?
There is no escape in the midst of withdrawals,
It has you exactly where it wants you.
In a stranglehold of desperation and desire,
For that one thing impossible to soothe it.
The drug of addiction now not an alternative.
So where do you go when addiction takes hold,
For there is no escape from the withdrawals,
When your mind feels shattered ,
Locked into the prison of both body and mind.
Other than death of course,
Suicidal ideation that comes with withdrawals.
There's always that option.
That itself is the pure truth of how utterly,
Distressing and destructive the reality of,
Addiction withdrawals really are.

The words drug addiction has so many,
Negative connotations quite rightly,
For drug addiction is a terrible condition.
But at my time of life it's even more awful,
In my minds eye it conjures up terrible sights,
Of which I cannot abide.
The revulsion I feel towards myself,
Is of a completely new kind.
Prescribed drug addiction has reduced,
Me to an utter baseness.
Of a type I never knew existed within myself.
An ugliness of human nature I'd have,
Related to Neanderthal man.
Not a civilised middle aged woman like I.
'Tis better I've learned, to say nothing of this.
For fear that people might think the worst,
That I'm some kind of junkie, a heroin addict.
No one assumes I'm withdrawing from,
A doctor that over prescribed,
Twenty times the amount of a drug for two
years.
That my addiction and withdrawals are,
The fault of one negligent doctor.
The sense of shame I feel is exceedingly real.
I wouldn't wish this experience on anyone,
This feeling of grubbiness, that lingers,
Around like a dirtiness that's impossible to
clean.
Scrubbing with bleach wouldn't touch this kind,
Of dirty stain all across my body and mind.
No scourer would remove this stain,
A constant reminder of my baseness.

Smothered by my Father,
Each and every way I turned,
Until the day that he died.
Smothered by my Father,
As a child one entity,
Is how we seemed.
No separate being was I,
For boundaries between him and I,
We're nonexistent.
I was he, he was I.
A childhood spent walking on,
Eggshells, frightened of falling.
Happened regardless of how,
Very careful I was.
The only winner was my Father.
Whatever Mind game he played,
He always won.
Twisted games of course,
I never stood a chance.
I understood the rules at five years,
Fifteen, twenty years.
That it was impossible for me to win.
Authoritarian control wins,
Hands down over a child,
Every single time. (Cont)

I grew up believing I was nothing,
Other than a loser, since,
Fair play was nonexistent,
In the household run by my Father,
The ultimate authoritarian control freak,
A mild description compared to the actual,
Truth of the Father he actually was. [32]

---

[32] There is nothing fair between the power of an adult compared to the powerlessness of a child. In this abusive situation the adult has all the strength, power and control.

I was a small, pale, sickly child,
That failed to thrive.
Although no one understood why of course,
Least of all I.
Illnesses seemed to haunt me.
One following another closely.
Taking twice as long to recover,
Than either my brother or sister.
I was frightened of taking medicines,
For they tasted quite disgusting,
Inside my mouth,
I'd have trouble swallowing it,
Every single time.
Unaware then that this fear,
Was inextricably linked to the abuse.
Only knowing I irritated her,
Annoying my Father,
Making swallowing anything,
A thousand times more difficult,
Particularly with tears, [33]
Streaming down my face.

---

[33] My Father was disgusted by my crying. He used to tell me to "turn off the taps, you won't get any sympathy from me young lady". It's very difficult as a young child to learn self-control.

A childhood spent chained to my Father,
Sexually, physically, mentally and emotionally.
A child in a serpents venomous den.
Unable to understand the reality of my life.
I knew not why I was the chosen child,
The one of three, required to suffer in silence.
Nothing makes sense when you're a young child,
Living in an adult world of complex suffering.
Imagining reasons to justify my childhood,
Which as a child I found necessary,
In order to survive.
Illogical reasoning that made sense then,
Although not now of course.
To live in the reality of the venomous den,
To justify the snakes behaviours.
Telling myself repeatedly that it was,
Of course all my own fault.
That I deserved to be treated this way,
That without a doubt I deserved,
Everything that I got.
To suffer such behaviours, I understood,
I was utterly worthless and unlovable.
That was the Child that I was,
Punishable for being unlovable.

It took a whole decade in captivity,
To learn how to feel again,
To understand the meaning of feelings.
For as a young child my Father,
Stripped me of all my feelings,
Saying only adults had the right to,
Self-expression of all kinds.
I couldn't cry, I'd forgotten how,
Fear I remembered.
Joy was a complete mystery to me,
As were most other feelings.
I wasn't encouraged to think for myself,
But to follow my Fathers authoritarian rules.
Anger absolutely terrified me.
Learning how to feel and express,
Angry feelings took years.
And when it finally came the anger,
Swept through me like a tornado,
A tsunami, a lightning bolt,
In waves that crashed ceaselessly,
For a time through my mind, my body and soul,
So powerful I learned to master,
Self-control, unlike my Father had.

Shame was without a doubt,
My greatest stumbling block of all.
Taking considerable time to articulate,
To understand it's enormity within me.
To recognise its roots in my tangled childhood.
Then to believe in my own childhood,
Innocence, rather than guilt.
After blaming myself for year after year.
Reverse thinking wasn't easy.
Logic was what made it clearer.

Father being a fully grown adult,
An irresponsible man that he was then.
Shame had filled every single cell in my body,
Disgust at myself totally inappropriate.
It took a long time to accept this as true,
To accept myself as not to blame,
For the childhood atrocities,
That traumatised me as a child.
To accept that I was blameless as a child,
When now a fully drown woman,
Was harder than one could ever imagine.
To change my thinking,
To a more positive powerful view of my being.
There was no easy fix to this trauma.
Recovery takes time and there is no,
Magic wand available,
To turn what was a living nightmare, (cont…)

Into something I could deal with.
I turned these thoughts around and around,
Inside my exhausted mind.
Validation helped, bringing with it clarity.
A different perspective,
Brought on by hindsight as an adult.
The result was a clearer understanding,
Of who I was and why.
Self-identity came last, [34]
Based on the Past,
Newly reinstated in the Present,
Enabling me a Future of some kind,
Forgiving but not forgotten,
That's the way it was.
For I was no longer a victim,
But a Survivor,
A Warrior Woman.

---

[34] In this life there are two choices, to be a victim or a survivor. I got sick of being the victim, and chose recovery in order to be a Survivor.

It was years since I'd cried,
Literally forgotten the natural process.
I'd reached the point where crying,
Even if I wanted too, never occurred.
I'd learned my Fathers lessons well as a child.
It reached the stage where others,
Believed that I was cold, unfeeling.
Difficult then to explain,
What I then couldn't even explain to myself
The unexplainable.
They called me the Ice Queen.
I'd have thought the same in their shoes.
Didn't solve the problem though,
Childhood amnesia and all that.
Eventually I became terrified of crying,
The idea of loss of control frightening.
What if once I'd started I couldn't stop?
So I tightened my smiling mask,
And held myself together.
Finally I learned to cry once more,
Behind the locked doors of the Asylum.
Years later, this was, the tears,
Once started hardly abated.
I cried Oceans in the Asylum,
To begin with I despised myself for crying,
Hated this weakness of mine,
Until I learned it was a, (cont...)

Natural bodily function.
It was then that my shame,
Finally dispersed,
When I understood the purpose of crying,
That it relieved some of my blocked feelings.
That crying can bring with it a kind of relief,
And knowing then,
That I was no longer the Ice Queen.

There is no equivalent to utter misery.
It consumes your entire body, mind and soul.
Reducing you to nothing other,
Than tears, pain and every baseline feeling,
In between.
A maze of desperate feelings tangled together.
Tightly interwoven and indistinct,
From each other.
Unbelievably distressing in both their,
Depth and breadth,
Leaving you staggering and breathless,
Smothered and suffocating in a quagmire of,
Unabated uncontrollable feelings,
Of the most intense and frightening kind.
Unknowing as to whether,
This torrential downpour would ever abate,
Respond to reason, or finally stop,
Long enough for me to catch my breath,
For my misery seemed exponential,
Suffering.

In the midst of depression,
Any views are obscured by the,
Darkest darkness,
Like thick black ominous clouds.
Standing alone in my darkest times,
With no Future before me,
And the Past long gone,
Darkness clings to my body,
Wrapping it's poisonous tendrils,
Tightly around me.
Inside and outside it holds me,
Prisoner,
Paralysing me with lethargy.
Deep exhaustion and apathy.
Without any visible light to see,
There is no lightness of being,
Only a heaviness,
As solid and heavy as concrete.
Weighing me down,
Like harsh gravity,
Pining me to my own bed.
That is the weight of,
Deepest darkest depression.

My Father might well have had a,
Samurai sword and sliced me through my,
Middle, head to feet,
With one lightening strike.
Through the top of my skull,
Down to my vagina.
As it was he ripped me apart.
With his bare hands,
His mockery and sarcasm,
Sexual abuse,
Physical violence,
Emotional blackmail,
Mental cruelty.
"Tis true it would have been easier,
Let alone quicker,
To have used a Samurai sword.
One clean slice and I'd have been,
Put out of my misery far sooner. [35]

---

[35] I sometimes thought that had I been an animal I would have
been put out of my suffering in a humane way.

A newborn baby is an innocent being.
If you e ever held one,
You'll know exactly what I mean.
Each newborn baby,
Enters this world with nothing.
Innocence defined.
Marred in no way at all,
Unblemished by knowledge,
Or experiences and into a world,
Where Nature versus Nurture.
That's what they say,
The geneticists, psychologists, educationalists.
And if this really is the truth,
Then Nurture failed me totally.
Within my first five years,
My innocence had been stolen,
And trampled upon.
What followed were childhood nightmares,
Rampaging through the darkness of night.
A newborn baby is an innocent being,
Until Nurture of the worst kind,
Intervenes stealing innocence forever,
Thus stripping the child of,
It's innocent Nature. [36]

---

[36] All children are innocent without any exceptions. Children do not ask to be abused. It is never the child's fault. It is always the adults.

It is impossible to save another human being.
For we all live within our bodies and minds.
Tangled inside his own contorted mind,
My Father being a prime example,
My Father was irresponsible yet responsible,
For his own wrongdoings.
Our uniqueness makes us separate beings,
It's impossible to experience the,
Absolute truth of another's experiences.
I could never have walked in my Fathers shoes,
In a futile attempt to understand him.
For its impossible to learn what motivates,
Another, especially a Father to abuse,
His own daughter.
To understand my Fathers mind,
Was utterly beyond my comprehension.
Imagination tells me that his own mind,
Existed as his own personal hellfire.
That logic and reason played little part,
In my Fathers torturous attentions towards me.

Abuse of all kinds,
Cannot be reduced to reason and logic,
Particularly in relation,
To a Father to daughter,
Abusive relationship,
There clearly is no sufficient answer,
To the mind of any abuser.
And in the end, I could only save myself.
Unwritten words tell us and others nothing.
Nothing of the trauma of childhood abuse.
Nothing of the following teenage years,
Spent bullied and in isolation.
Nothing of the younger adult years,
Spent desperately trying to,
Hold oneself together.
Nothing of the terror of a decade in the Asylum,
Or the exponential infinite,
Abandonment issues.
Nothing of the assaults or rape that followed,
Or the egocentric bastard of a,
Consultant Psychiatrist.
Nor the dank, damp, dark, decaying,
Living environment, the Asylum.
Nothing of the decade spent there,
And the five that followed in other Institutions.
Or of the multiple diagnoses,
Nothing of the homelessness or the,
Rampant institutionalisation.
Or my final walk to freedom.
Nothing of the birth of my daughter,
Born with a serious heart defect.
Or the traumatic birth of my son seven years on.
Nothing of the fibromyalgia,

That left me a single disabled mother.
Or the doctor that grossly over prescribed me,
The resulting addiction and withdrawals.
Nor the more recent hospital admissions,
Resulting from the withdrawals.
Unwritten words tell one nothing.
I have opened my inner world to you,
In the hope that by explaining,
The total effects of mental illnesses,
From their origin to recovery,
I might in some small way raise awareness,
Of mental health issues.
Raising awareness of subjects,
Too often not discussed.
Demonstrating the impact of mental illness,
So others might understand.
I have barred my soul for you, for me,
In order to understand the full detrimental,
Effects mental illnesses,
Have had throughput my entire life,
Too date.

However wise one believes they are,
Doesn't really matter at all.
At the end of each and every day,
Intelligence or aptitude do not play,
Much part in matters of the heart.
Most important is without a doubt,
Emotional intelligence,
The ability to understand and relate to,
Another's point of view.
To react with compassion and understanding,
In an empathic way.
Some of the cleverest people I've ever met,
Have often lacked in emotional understanding.
Thus finding it important to relate to others,
Or to imagine themselves in another's shoes.
These days I'll go with emotional intelligence,
Always in favour over a high IQ.
There are of course those with both,
A high IQ and emotional intelligence.
My Father was highly intelligent,
Yet without any emotional intelligence,
That I experienced or could see.
The facet of his character that destroyed my,
Childhood.
A high IQ alone did not make my,
Father a good parent, a good father.(cont..)

His lack of emotional intelligence, in my eyes,
Made him a cruel and devastating parent.
One with no feelings whatsoever. [37]
My Father was impossible to relate to,
In every single possible way.
My Father failed as a parent,
That much is definitely true.

---

[37] Emotional intelligence is probably more important than a high
IQ. The ability to show compassion, empathy and understanding in
today's world are exceedingly important.

Youth was spent with my head in the clouds,
The great dark clouds of depression.
Weighing heavily upon my stooped shoulders,
My whole demeanour lost in a haze of misery.
My childhood was the same of course.
Though then I'd not heard of the word,
'Depression '.
Life eventually transpired into the,
Nightmare world of the old lunatic Asylum.
After which all was completely lost.
Throughout the entire decade that followed.
Only worse of course for the Depression clouds,
Then proceeded to swallow me whole,
Tipping me headfirst into the bottomless pit,
That was the Abyss.
It took years to break free and recover,
Which only occurred after a personal decision,
That enough was enough.

That I was in the End absolutely sick and tired,
Of being trapped within the,
Mental health system.
All it had proved in the fifteen years,
Was that it had repeatedly failed me.
I wanted out, so I walked out.
Sixteen years ago now.
Believing I'd never return once more,
What a fool I was.(cont…)
But no one could have foreseen,
The negligent doctor,
Who turned me into a drug addict,
On far too high dose of,
Prescribed medication whereupon,
Addiction withdrawals,
Once more returned me to a,
Psychiatric Institution.

I'd like to have asked him,
What it felt like,
To reduce me to nothing.
To crush me between,
His finger and his thumb.
Whilst I was a young child,
He the adult.
Did he feel powerful?
Make him feel strong?
Dis he feel like a real man?
Crushing his small daughters,
Spirit and feelings,
Between his thumb and finger.
Like sand through a sieve,
That easy.
Did he enjoy it?
Watching me suffer.
The power he had,
To destroy his,
Daughter.
Yes,
I know he did.
For otherwise why do it.

A symbol of love.
The purity of a perfect rose.
It's colour crimson red.
The colour of blood.
Death and it's beauty wilts,
It sheds its petals,
To the ground, they gently fall.
Love is never perfect.
All human beings are flawed.
Feeling loved is a precious gift.
For the perfect dying rose,
For the human heart,
That without love feels as if,
It's bleeding till death.

Innocence,
Clean and pure,
Beautiful.
But,
Steal,
Innocence,
And it becomes,
Shamed and dirty.
Ugly,
Feelings,
Never forgotten.
For,
Once stolen,
Innocence violated,
Is infinitely impossible,
To replace.
These things are,
Never forgotten.
This was the,
Death,
Of,
Innocence,
And of Me.

Beauty is often only skin deep,
Appearances mean nothing,
We can be easily deceived.
For beauty lives in the Soul.
It's truth hidden deep from,
Immediate sight.
Look closer to find,
The truth of a,
Beautiful Soul,
Lives through the,
Fathomless depths,
Of our eyes.

I was a Child,
Then a Teenager,
Finally an Adult woman.
But somewhere in Time,
I stopped growing up.
Stunted emotionally,
Mentally and physically.
By the forgotten destruction,
Of my lost childhood,
Traumatic amnesia,
Made it so difficult to function.
Without memories,
No understanding of why,
I was the messed-up woman that I was,
Floundering in a labyrinth,
Of misunderstanding.
Caught in a spiders web of self-destructive,
Overwhelming thoughts.
Without any idea of how I'd gotten,
Into the mess of Me,
Then Past,
Present Past,
No future did I see.

My Father used mockery and sarcasm,
To belittle, to undermine my feelings repeatedly.
Every single feeling I felt became a joke.
Justified because apparently I couldn't,
Wouldn't take a joke or teasing.
He said, 'words don't hurt'.
Truth is words can be utterly devastating,
Breaking ones heart repeatedly.
Words can be shaming and disgusting,
Until the only feelings left are those that leave,
You feeling completely worthless.
Where believing oneself invisible,
Is better than feeling anything.
Whilst dying a slow protracted death,
Inside and outside,
Is the only feeling remaining,
In your body, soul and mind.
Where death is preferable,
To living as a joke,
Repeatedly shamed and humiliated. [38]

---

[38] Shaming and humiliation, mockery and sarcasm are very effective ways of destroying a child. There is nothing worse than every feeling being mocked and invalidated for destroying a child's psyche.

A head full of misinformation,
Authoritarian delivered,
Ultimatums, rules and regulations.
Followed by frightened,
Silent submission,
Avoiding punishment.
Reassessment of misinformation,
Difficult at best after continual brainwashing.
To the point of having no other thoughts,
Thoughts that belong to yourself alone.
Different from those thoughts,
That belonged to my Father.
Who told me that only adults,
Had the right to think,
For themselves.
And that was not I,
Not back then.

A Child should be a Child,
Not treated as a woman,
Or worse a piece of butchers meat.
A Child is not a Woman,
Childhood is short enough as it is.
By stealing my childhood,
My Father violating me as he did,
Treated me instead as a woman.
It's utterly unacceptable,
That any child should be treated this way.
Sexual abuse of children,
Is always criminally inappropriate.
By abusing my innocence,
My childhood innocence,
By using my body sexually.
My Father was violating his own child,
His daughter.
Abusing my Rights.
Innocence stolen.
Childhood ruined.
Traumatic experiences.
Post traumatic stress disorder.
A crime and a sin.
For I was never his woman.
Only ever his innocent Child.

The Origins of Evil.
A fascinating question.
Difficult to establish or understand.
Just as difficult to provide a,
Coherent answer to.
In any comprehensible way.
I trained as a school teacher,
Before the Asylum.
Taught young children,
And can quite categorically say,
Young children are not born evil,
It's society that makes some this way.
Our environment,
The way we Nurture,
Bring up our own children.
The society that we live in effects,
Us all in different ways.
The minds of young children,
Growing to become adults,
Each experiencing their lives differently.
Every child born, is born innocent,
We need to look outside ourselves,
If innocence turns to evil.
To consider the way society influences us,
For therein lies the truth. (Cont…)

Our environment, our education,
Our surroundings, our homes.
All play an important part in the way,
We age and grow up.
Evil isn't born, it's created,
By the World and people around us,
Nothing more, nothing less. [39]

---

[39] The smiling mask of depression is part of the reason that stigma still exists. The rise of self-harm, suicides, and depression in teenagers particularly are an indication that these subjects are still not being openly discussed and dealt with.

Strip the smiling masks of depression,
Free from our faces.
Reveal the vividness of feelings hidden,
For the convenience of others.
Strip the masks of our faces.
Let those that are ignorant,
Turning their backs,
Be faced with the truth,
Of our suffering.
Strip the mask of our faces,
So that they may be forced to acknowledge,
The truth of who we really are.
Time and time again.
Refuse to hide our personal realities,
Displaying the truth of our existence,
In full lucidity vividly.
Let them see the pain and the suffering,
That they are so mortally afraid of.
Refuse to hide the truth,
Let them feel their discomfort,
At witnessing pain and suffering.
For our masks merely prolong our suffering,
So why hide it for the convenience of others,
From those too scared to face the reality,
Of mental illnesses.
It is our loss this hiding behind our masks,
Loss of time and healing. (Cont...)

We all deserve better.
Much better than hiding behind our masks,
Purely for the convenience of others,
Right?
It's the only way to End the Stigma. [40]

---

[40] The smiling mask of depression is part of the reason that stigma still exists. The rise of self-harm, suicides, and depression in teenagers particularly are an indication that these subjects are still not being openly discussed and dealt with.

My Father only wore his mask outside our
house.
Never wore it inside, his feelings,
Always blatantly visible.
Especially to his young daughter.
The frightened young child that I was then.
As I grew older I became more aware,
Of the differences between my Father,
In the outside world,
As apposed to life behind the,
Closed doors of our family home.
I began then to understand the utter hypocrisy,
Of his existence, a two faced bastard.
Where were his ethics and morals?
That he was so desperate to enforce,
Throughout my childhood.
Spending so much time telling me not to lie.
But whilst he was lying all that time?
Pretending to be open minded.
Whilst behind closed doors,
He was a total racist, homophobic too.
Liar, liar, liar.
Tell the truth, he always insisted,
Whilst lying through his teeth.
I was fifteen years old,
Before I discovered his duplicity.
Before I discovered,
What an utter hypocrite,
My Father actually was all that time.

Prescribed drug addiction withdrawals,
From excessive amounts of lorazepam daily.
Tow years of taking twenty milligrams a day.
Resulting in short-term memory loss.
Causing utter distress and frustration.
Cant remember faces, places.
What I've said, what I haven't.
My mind is a void of blank nothingness.
Feeling as if I have dementia at my age.
Longterm use of benzodiazepines,
Can apparently cause short term memory loss.
Frustration and distress at,
Repeating the same information,
Time and time again that I've already,
Said the same thing ten times previously.
Then there are the awkward embarrassing,
Moments faced with people that know me,
I stand and stare with no recollection,
Of ever meeting them before.
I feel embarrassed and ashamed,
At my total lack of recognition.
I'm not a stupid person,
But these drug withdrawals make me feel,
That way and far far worse still.

Addiction the darkness within.
Scraping my insides filthy.
It's claws as sharp as a steel knife,
Cutting through reason and logic.
Like nails scraping down a chalk board.
Anxiety spiking repeatedly like lightening m
The thunder reverberating within.
Migraines clawing my mind.
Nausea cramping my insides.
Sickness rising in my throat.
Taste of metallic bile.
Shaky hands, spasms that rack my limbs,
Like a puppet on a string this time,
Dancing to the tune of,
Addiction withdrawals.
Anxiety buzzing inside my head,
Making my thinking unclear.
Overwhelming feelings and,
Suicidal thinking making addiction,
And it's withdrawals,
Far too much to bear.

I cannot abide those that make,
False Promises.
Those that lie because it makes,
Their lives, their jobs easier.
All my life I've been abandoned and lied too.
You'd think at my age people would,
Show a little more respect, but so many fail too.
Instead they continually mess me around,
To the point that now, I turn my back on them.
They are time wasters and life is short enough.
So many make promises that the probably,
Know they'll never keep.
Mind games aren't for me I prefer,
To get absolutely straight to the point, clearly.
It saves so much time, without room,
For misunderstandings.
I wish people would think before they spoke,
Think about their words,
And the potential damage to others,
Should their promises be impossible to keep.
A lot less damage would be done,
And a lot more time saved.

Time is the only constant in our lives,
Moving us on relentlessly throughout,
Our lives birth until death.
In directions we choose, or those that we don't.
Time moves forwards constantly.
So much of my own life from childhood,
Through to adulthood, hasn't been the choice,
I myself would have made back then.
Childhood trauma and associated memories,
Complicated my life then, and after then.
So many of the choices in my life,
We're choices made for me by my Father.
Then by the Consultant Psychiatrist,
In the Asylum.
Both these men forced their own decisions,
About my life on to me.
Their own opinions and views.
Two authoritarian alpha males,
Both ignorant and arrogant.
Neither showed any compassion, empathy,
And certainly no understanding.
By the age of eight, my Father had stolen,
Both my innocence and identity,
Leaving me feeling completely worthless.
By eight I already knew instinctively,
It was too late, I was already broken.
There is this saying,
'Give me a child until he is seven and I,(cont...)

Will give you the man', a quote that,
Has stood the test off time.
By eight it was already too late for me.
I was on a path that I'd not chosen.
Much of what happened in the years afterwards,
Was mostly predictable, sadly.
My first real decision was to walk out of,
Psychiatric mental health services.
My second decision was to have my daughter,
To become a single mother.
I made these choices including seven years,
Later to have my son.
For time is relentless, marching forward.
Use it wisely before it is too late,
To do anything worthwhile at all.
Time doesn't wait for any man or woman,
So don't wait for the right time,
For the right time is now.

I've always felt like a half sketched person,
Since as a child I had no sense of self-identity.
There were no boundaries that,
Separated my Father and I.
There were no feelings that I could express,
For as a child my Father forbade feelings.
A half-sketched child, teenager and adult.
No colour, mostly invisible, no real depth.
When I was much younger,
I often felt completely out of my depth,
In the adult world of rules and feelings,
I felt worthless, didn't know how to be.
A quiet child, submissive, often silent.
If this taught my anything,
It taught me how to listen, how to hear.
But during my childhood years,
So much of my emotional understanding,
Was utterly deficient and wanting.
Feeling some resemblance to a 'whole' person,
Only occurred on becoming a mother myself.
As a 'Mother' I became a whole new identity,
A person others could relate too.
An identity I could always relate too. [41]

---

[41] I never felt as if I was a whole person. I had no sense of identity myself.

Darkest depression how I loathe you.
All those years that you have haunted my life,
Following closely at my heels,
Shadowing my length continually.
From childhood to adulthood you've doggedly,
Pursued me throughout my life.
Depressed and distressed me ceaselessly,
Falling and climbing in and out of the abyss.
Falling and climbing, falling and climbing,
Into and out of the deepest darkest,
Bottomless Abyss.
So much of my life spent in the darkness,
The result of traumatic experiences.
Fighting the desire to die, or not to die,
Relentlessly and repeatedly.
Exhausting battles between body, mind and
soul.
Weakening my survival mechanisms,
More each and every single time.
Death and depressive have walked by my side,
My entire life through, just waiting,
Waiting for the right time to finally take me.
Deepest darkest depression, how I hate you.
I have no doubt that you will,
Shadow my life right up until it's end.
I will never be entirely free of you.
You are a parasite within me,
And I cannot gouge you out of me,
That you are never welcome doesn't bother,
You in the slightest, you are always ready,
To jump aboard, turning my life again,
Towards misery. (Cont)

You wait beside me patiently, waiting,
For me to stumble, to trip, to fall,
Once again into the bottomless pit of depression.
That you are always so close by,
Makes me despise you forever more.
I hate you deepest darkest depression,
And I always will do.

Missing parts, missing pieces,
Lost in the depths and darkness of childhood.
Some pieces permanently lost,
Whilst over time others were regained.
Never the whole person, for that, I never was.
Impossible to regain something,
Never experienced, not then, not now.
You cannot violate a child,
Then expect them to grow up whole.
When there are pieces missing,
Memories and experiences.
Mostly not remembered but baring,
A stark resemblance,
To shrapnel wounds, or bullet holes,
Fired from a high speed machine gun,
Peppering holes in my entire childhood.
Leaving behind the collateral damage
Forgotten memories, a broken psyche.
It's impossible to make such a person,
Whole again, in every sense of the words or a,
Traumatised child , teenager and adult ,
Can never become what they never were.
A sense of wholeness, a stable identity,
An unsurprising impossibility.
I was far too young when the trauma began.
Too young to understand anything.
Least of all the damage that was being done,
To me then, and the impact it would have, later.

Death came to visit me, riding on horseback.
In the deepest darkest hour of the night.
Death came with the determination,
Of the Cavaliers on horseback.
Thundering hooves kicked back dirt.
Death arrived, no introduction required.
Death stared at I, I stared at Death,
Both of us waiting for the other to move first.
We stood like this for awhile,
At the edge of the World.
Death on horseback, whilst I stood still,
Looking up, looking down.
Then I turned aside.
In that fleeting moment I heard Death move,
A cloud of dust, thundering hooves.
Death rode away, not one glance back,
For Death and I were old friends.
We both knew that sooner or later,
We'd both meet yet again.
Sooner, later, sooner.

Trapped by birth in a childhood of trauma.
Unable to escape its confines and confusion,
Of my body, my mind and of my soul.
Trapped inside myself, inside my mind,
Inside my home, inside my Father.
The confines of my life not understood.
Overwhelming feelings,
Terrifying traumatic experiences.
Trapped in my home environment,
Unable to understand what was happening.
Freedom was never an option for a child like I,
A child at the mercy of a Father,
Without compassion,
Understanding or empathy.
Trapped inside my childhood terrors,
Overwhelming fears of suffocation both,
Physically and emotionally.
Finding absolutely no way out,
Trapped is a feeling I've so often had.
In my childhood and teenage years,
And as an adult locked inside,
The claustrophobic confines of the Asylum.
Abandoned and lonely,
Trapped with overwhelming overthinking,
Suicidal thoughts and feelings.
Trapped within myself.

When I'm silent yet screaming inside,
My mind becomes the locked gate to my voice.
Sometimes the gate explodes outwards,
And rage streams out of my mouth.
Not often in my life have I lost my temper,
Yet when I do, the rage feels like fire.
At injustices and traumas beyond my control.
Frustration boils over until the internal,
Pressure cooker inside my mind,
Screeches for release of some kind at,
The egotistical bastard,
That was my Consultant Psychiatrist,
At the negligent doctor that destroyed my life,
And the mental health system that,
Almost always continues to fail.
These are a few of the things that enrage me.
Sometimes it's better to express anger,
Rather than bottle it up like a cancerous parasite,
Eating away at my mind, my brain tissue alive.
Sometimes anger is appropriate,
Under circumstances that have left me suffering,
Traumatised and hurting.

Convergent light, divergent light,
Reflected in my eyes.
Reflections of my childhood.
Refractive light, protracted light,
Reflections of my teens.
Darkest night, without any light,
Terrifying sights to be seen.
Reflections of my life.
Do not stare into my eyes,
Do not search for my Soul,
If pain and suffering isn't acceptable.
Where ignorance is bliss.
Preferable to this.
Do not stare into my Soul,
If you have no compassion, lack empathy,
Especially no real understanding.
Do not stare into my Soul,
If you're intolerant to the truth.
Instead, look deeper into your own Soul.

It's far easier to build up a child,
Than it is to repair an adult.
Those that violate and destroy children,
Like my own Father,
Abandoning his broken daughter,
To survive and consequently to fight,
For her own life.
I found recovery an immense uphill journey,
To recover from a childhood of trauma,
And lacking so many baseline skills.
As a parent myself and a school teacher,
I know and understand that,
Childhood is the time where children learn,
All those social skills required by schools.
All those things relied on in later life,
Trust, love, joy and a degree of self-worth,
Identity, confidence and self-esteem.
If instead, as my own childhood was,
There are a series of traumatic experiences,
Instead, so many of these things are lost,
Or were never there.
Making recovery as an adult far more complex,
Since the basic building blocks,
Of childhood development were clearly missing.
With no confidence, esteem, worthiness,
Recovering as an adult,
Was for me exceedingly difficult,
Though not impossible.

We are the new generation.
A society that depends far more on,
Antidepressants than ever before in our history.
Is this not a reflection of a society that fails,
Care about individuals anymore.
Whose children and teenagers are the most,
Unhappy, where self-harm and depression,
Have reached all time highs,
So many of us dependent on antidepressants.
Pharmaceutical companies making,
So much money from our unhappiness,
Antidepressants taken in the hope of,
Feeling human, feeling stable.
Such a society surely reflects a lack of,
Basic understanding of the way stresses in life.
Not recognising that so many of us are suffering,
Due to a lack of compassion and empathy.
The fast technological world we live in,
Often forgets we are all individuals.
We may be a technological advanced society ,
Yet we're also emotionally neglectful of the,
Youths so often suffering in silence,
In a society that seems so often to acknowledge,
That it has a problem, depression,
At an all time high, reflecting unhappiness.
Nothing will change until society acknowledges,
The damage it's doing to each new generation.
It doesn't matter how many,
Protective layers you grow, layer after layer,
Cannot protect you from the truth within.

Sometimes self protection,
Is completely and utterly impossible.
Sexual, physical, mental and emotional abuse,
Traumatic experiences,
Violations of the body and soul,
These penetrate every single defensive layer.
Offering no real protection at all.
Even though I built a fortress around myself,
So high that no one could possibly climb over,
No one could reach me I'd thought,
And I couldn't climb out to freedom resulted,
In my becoming utterly detached and silent.
Depersonalisation made me unreachable,
Even to myself, within myself.
The metaphorical wall was tall and sturdy.
No door, no window, no ladder, nothing,
With which I could escape my own prison.
Nothing that allowed others in either.
I filled this void with coldness,
Colder than a Siberian winters howling winds.
It took years to demolish this wall,
So that I could get out, others get in,
Took years to open myself to being hurt again.

Body shaming,
Hating, disgracing.
Disgusting, dirty, violations,
Of body and trust.
Dissociating, denting, disbelieving,
Body ownership rights invisible.
Tainted, broken, damaged goods,
On sale according to my Father.
Self-hatred of the venomous kind.
Unforgiving towards myself.
Blaming my body, myself, for the,
Violations, the violence.
Worthless child, teenager, and adult.
Cheap and used, damaged and broken,
In mind, body and spirit.

I spent my childhood living in the shadows,
The Shadowlands.
No more than a small shadow of a child.
Blending in was easier,
Easier than the unwanted attention,
Of my Father.
Including those that I didn't understand,
Those that didn't understand me either.
Not that I ever fitted in anywhere,
Not throughout my childhood,
Teenager years or young adulthood.
I was nothing more than a,
Shadow girl.
Blending in with each environment,
Like a chameleon taking cover.
Most people never actually saw me,
A flicker perhaps in their peripheral vision.
A blink of an eye and I was long gone.
With no feelings of self-identity,
I hid myself in the shadows,
For far more years than not.
Comfortable with my shadow,
Not with others.
There was a small degree of safety,
Of protection, living in the,
Shadowlands around me.

Nightmares and night terrors,
Fuelled by addiction withdrawals.
Horrific scenes of chaos and carnage.
Scenes I've never even imagined before,
Surreal to the extreme.
Waking up shaky and sweating,
Three thirty in the morning.
Exhausted from so few hours sleep.
Invaded by beings unimaginably terrible.
Too frightened to sleep again.
Sitting alone in the silence of the early hours,
Sleep now no longer the escape it once had been.
Instead I'm left feeling trapped inside,
These nightmares, night terrors.
Leaving me constantly exhausted.
Addiction withdrawals,
Awful and disabling.

There are too many words inside my head.
Most of which I don't want to hear.
Overwhelming overthinking,
Suicidal ideation plague my mind,
Relentlessly.
If I could I'd cut them out just to silence them,
These self-destructive thoughts of mine.
I'd rather silence than this white noise,
Screaming inside my mind.
I didn't ask for this life of mine,
So much of which was beyond my control.
I didn't actually ask to be born,
For the childhood trauma and abuse,
That followed, or the,
Teenage years of depression and misery.
All these choices were made by my Father.
Wanting the impossible, perfection.
Abandoning me in the Asylum,
Fifteen years in Institutions.
I've tried to sort it out,
The mess he made of me.
And just as I thought I was stable,
Came fibromyalgia disabling me.
Followed by the negligent doctor,
The one that turned me into a drug addict.
Then came the horrendous withdrawals,
Four hospital admissions,
Leaving me more unstable than ever.
I'm more than my body,
Though for most of my life,
I've not believed so.
Sexual abuse as a child,
No boundaries or self-identity.

Fear of being touched,
Disgust at my own body,
Left believing that my body,
Belonged to my Father.
Then other men followed.
Without boundaries,
I misunderstood.
My body was for me I'd been told,
Id believed my Father for years.
Because it certainly felt that way.
It was exceedingly hard,
To then learn that my body was my own,
That the sexual abuse wasn't my fault,
That boundaries had to be learned.
A long hard lesson, taking years,
To put right what was so wrong.
Of convincing and believing,
That I deserved better,
After the trauma of my childhood.
That my body belonged to me alone,
That I'm more than flesh and bone.
Took time, so much time,
Longer than you could possibly imagine.
I'm the Joker, you said.
But I never found him funny.
You can't take a joke, he said.
Reducing me to tears.
Such a silly girl, he'd say.
The shame I felt too much.

It's only a bloody joke, he stated.
I tried to stop crying, really.
For crying out loud, he shouted!
I move backwards in my seat,
Dissociating,
Waiting to be struck.
He didn't understand my Father.
That his jokes, aimed at me personally,
Weren't funny at all.
His words hurt and shamed me.
Then making me feel foolish,
He'd say irritated,
You're so bloody hypersensitive!
I wince at the degradation in his voice.
Take a bloody joke girl!
You need to toughen up!
Turn off the tears,
If you can't take a bloody joke.,
Then just get out of my sight girl!
I moved before he could think twice,
Gone in a flash still sobbing.
His mockery and sarcasm, (cont….)
Thinly disguised as jokes with hindsight.
These jokes were always directed at me,
I never found his attempts at humour,
Funny, for his words repeatedly,
Shamed me.
I hated being laughed at,
His criticisms and cruelty for this,
Joker, wasn't funny,
Even if he believed he was.
He most certainly wasn't in my eyes.

All the colours,
Of the Rainbow seeped,
Out of my childhood.
Until in the end there was only,
Black and white like a chequer board.
No colours at all.
My Father of course was the King,
I was a lowly pawn,
In each game he insisted on playing.
He won each and every time,
With a kind of manic glee.
Satisfied that,
Every single move he made,
Forwards, backwards, diagonally,
He would always outmanoeuvre me.
I never stood a chance.
Taking my down painfully fast,
As fast as he possibly could.
The Grand Chess Master.
Excellent at mind games,
Was a master at the art,
Of totally destroying,
Me in every single way.
The Grand Chess Master,
Was diabolically,
Cruel.

It's four in the morning,
Awake and shaking.
Nightmares that repeat themselves,
Like an old news reel,
Around and around,
Leaving me exhausted,
Yet unable to sleep.
I sit and stare at nothing,
Feeling the stillness,
Of the early hours once more.
Never have I felt so alone,
Than during these solitary hours,
With only the ticking clock,
For company,
Soon even this becomes an,
Utter irritation.

All I want is more than four,
Hours sleep each night.
Sleep free from,
Withdrawal nightmares,
Those that continually haunt me.
Never have I felt so,
Exhausted.
Never had death felt so near.
I sit alone in the silence,
Waiting for the new day,
Tears sliding down my cheeks,
Knowing not what to do.
The cost of silence is unimaginable.
Collateral damage grows at an exponential rate,
During almost three decades of silence.
Silence only suits the abuser,
Not the abused.
Silence is a form of slow suicide,
Eating away at ones insides.
Claiming your life with all the,
Misinformation and misunderstandings,
Of a child. (Cont)

Untangling the truth means breaking,
The silence, speaking out.
Only through speaking of these things,
Do we make recovery possible.
To be validated, to understand finally,
That we're not to blame,
Enables relief and a sense of freedom.
The weight of the burden carried for years,
Is finally lifted and moved to the right place,
The abuser, not the abused.
Speaking out is the only way,
To dig out the truth,
From the open infected wounds.
It is the truth that will eventually,
Set you free.

Faded,
Jaded childhood.
Shadowlands of,
Sorrow.
Darkest darkness,
Was Darkness.
Silent days of,
Solitude.
Long grey days,
Whatever the,
Season.
Traumatic,
Experiences.
Suffocating,
Stillness.
Dissociating,
Desperately,
Despite not,
Understanding.
Unhappiness an,
Understatement as a,
Child.
Blending with the,
Shadowlands of our,
Victorian family home.

Post traumatic stress disorder.
Endless consequences,
Throughout my entire life.
Particularly in relation to,
The opposite sex.
Relationships being impossible,
To sustain.
Due to that feeling within me,
From long ago childhood days,
That my body is being used,
Therefore it's being abused.
Difficulty in trusting men.
Childhood stemmed,
Sometimes difficult to,
Convince myself still,
That I'm more than just a body,
Fathers teachings,
Echo from the,
Deep and distant Past. [42]

---

[42] Complex Post traumatic stress disorder disorder is a condition that never leaves you. It's left me hyper vigilant and easily startled. I have excellent hearing and when out see and hear everything that moves or makes a sound. My body is constantly alert for any sign of danger.

High anxiety state relentlessly,
Causing uncertainty and fear.
The withdrawals are continuing to,
Hold me hostage in every single way.
My hands shake, my nerves frayed.
Anxiety buzzing inside my head.
Until I'm jumping at every slight movement,
At Every single sound,
Anxiety driving me round the bend,
With its relentless symptoms,
None of which I'd ever recommend.
Anxiety is a stress killer. [43]

---

[43] Extreme anxiety can be as disabling as depression. Stress is a well known killer. Panic attacks that feel like heart attacks are extreme scary.

You want to look inside my head?
All you'll see is an utter mess.
Tangled feelings, words and thoughts,
In no particular order.
Dead places in the grey matter,
Withered and died as a result of trauma.
Voids, empty spaces, nothing remembered.
Gaps in my childhood I still cannot fill.
You still want to look inside my head?
Don't say I didn't warn you.
If you're looking for my soul, I'm sorry,
It's out of order or I lost it, not sure which.
Untangling the entire mess,
Is a complete impossibility so I've given up.
No point in delving too deep,
Into such an utter mess.
There are so many missing pieces,
That coupled with my short-term memory loss,
It's hardly worth the bother, is it.
So turn off the light you're shining,
Inside my head, and consider this?
It's impossible to mend absolutely everything,
All that's broken, all that shattered.
So save yourself the trouble,
Concentrate on the Present instead.
For the Past has long since passed by,
Long since gone,
All that's left is the Present moment, now.
Overwhelming overthinking,
High functioning brain. (Cont)

It's caused me more trouble than,
You'd ever believe.
Continually questioning,
Re-questioning,
Diagnoses, medication,
Treatments.
Simpler if I'd kept my mouth shut.
Too many psychiatris prefer,
Submissive obedience to,
Open discussion and thinking.
Too many 'yes' patients,
Not enough 'no' patients.
Ethical and philosophical debates,
Not required.
University education hindered,
Rather than helped.
'Just do as youth told. I know what's best!'
Really, do you, I couldn't help thinking.
I doubted he did very much so.
Too many mistakes made by,
Professionals,
Who think they know,
The answers to all,
Yet fail to consider our uniqueness.
Herding us under one diagnosis,
Or the next, text book crap.

I never had a feeling of self-identity,
Not as a child or teenager.
My authoritarian father stamped,
Every last piece of me, from me.
When adulthood arrived I couldn't,
Identify anything of me.
So others stamped on me just as hard,
With much the same effect,
Repeatedly.
It's hard to be an adult with no identity.
Neither in childhood or beyond.
Everything I should have learned,
But hadn't.
The consequences were to repeat this,
Pattern for years afterwards.
Until I eventually learned to be me,
Regardless of the opinions of others,
And in spite of them.

Unseen mental illness,
Disguised from view by shame,
Fear of rejection, stigma, loneliness.
Invisible illnesses that twist your insides,
Turning you inside out, and back again.
Feelings so many don't understand,
Feelings not understood and feared,
Holding you back.
Suffering the effects of mental illness,
Throughout every part of your life.

Disabling you emotionally, socially,
Mentally and physically.
Sometimes more than one can bear.
Anxiety, depression, panic attacks,
And every other diagnoses.
None are pleasant, all of them hurt.
Disguising mental illness behind a smile,
Merely prolongs the suffering.
Asking for help and support,
Is the only way towards,
Recovery.

In the Asylum,
The egotistical bastard of a,
Consultant Psychiatrist,
Did everything he could,
To reduce me to utter silence,
To follow his rules, his thoughts,
Blindly and without question.
I did not comply.
I couldn't not after my Father.
Instead I debated my case,
Everything he said,
On every single occasion.
One of a kind, he'd sneer.
Clobbering me over the head,
With one Mental Health Section,
After another.
His ultimate power.
Which he used thirty-two times,
In a decade.
Reflecting how much he hated,
His views being questioned.[44]

---

[44] I had the same Consultant Psychiatrist for the entire decade. He used Mental Health Sectioning as freely as he used medication. In those 10 years he Sectioned me thirty-two times (sections 1, 2and 3 one after the other

We are all different people,
To different people.
Depending on the relationship.
Our characters are not linear,
But continually changing,
In response to our environment.
We grow or shrink inside,
Depending to whom we speak.
We are constantly changing within,
For we are learning, fitting-in,
Standing-out, loving, or not loving.
Adapting our personalities,
To that which we expect from ourselves.
Or to which others expect from us.
We are continually changing,
To meet the needs of,
Others and Ourselves.

I am not immune Death, to suffering,
Point blank range,
Would suit me perfectly.
Thank you for your,
Thoughtful consideration.
A quick death is absolutely essential.
But Death surely, there are other ways,
Of dying.
Ones that involve a little less blood,
And instead, offer eternal sleep?
For Death, I am utterly exhausted.
Truly.

Sometimes we scream in Silence,
Got to scream aloud would frighten us.
The very idea of losing self-control,
Terrifying.
All that uncontrollable anger, fury, fear,
Escaping from our Souls.
Like a banshees wailing, frightening,
In its utter intensity.
So me swallow down our screams,
Like bitter tasting medicines.
Creating havoc within us unleashed.
Feelings building up like an,
Internal pressure cooker,
With absolutely no where to go.
The more we swallow back our anger,
Our distress,
The more unwell we become.
Releasing our feelings is the only way,
For us to move on towards Recovery.
To the person we want to be.

Tears are a natural,
Human function.
Father despised my tears.
I learned to swallow,
Them down.
Past the tight knot,
In my throat.
Deep down and down.
Until I felt as if my body,
Was filled with all,
The Oceans of this,
World.

Hello Darkness, my old friend.
I see you Death.
Are you looking for me once more?
I'm still here waiting for you, as always.
I just haven't quite decided.
Death smiles at me, tips his hat.
Not quite ready, I respond.
Death considers me for a moment,
Then shrugs his money shoulders.
Pats me lightly on my back.
I'm a patient man, he says.
I know, I remember, this time I smile.
Death and I are old friends now.

My mind weighs more than I do.
A block of concrete inside my head.
I'd prefer a mind as light as a feather.
Uplifting thoughts rather than,
The enormous weight of depression.
It's an uphill struggle to achieve anything,
Whilst depressive symptoms weigh me down.
Overwhelming feelings weighing heavily,
On my shoulders causing lethargy.
I've forgotten how the lightness feels,
So long now have I been weighed down.
By all that is wrong and I'm struggling,
To feel a lightness of being is my dream.

Our Minds over time,
Have become a Science,
Psychological and accountable.
Our every feeling too easily,
Turned into a malady.
Not so before.
Every feeling we harbour,
Can be turned into a problem.
So much of what we feel,
Can be attributed,
To psychological problems.
Where once we were given a Tonic,
In order to relieve our symptoms.
Now it's pills and more pills,
I wonder if we e gone too far.
Turning every feeling,
Into something more than it is.
Scientific or Psychological,
Diagnoses.

My Father locked me inside his own had.
I was a prisoner of his own mind,
And thus a prisoner of my mind too.
He threw away the key to the lock,
When I was a young child.
Strict authoritarian behaviour ensured,
I couldn't have picked the lock,
Even had I been able.
I don't know why he locked me up like this,
But it effectively destroyed me.
Traumatic childhood experiences were,
Utterly silenced.
By the Jailor himself who understood,
All that I couldn't, and more so.
He showed no mercy in his behaviour,
Rather his power inflamed more,
Of the same behaviours.
My childhood and teenage years,
We're spent as a prisoner of the,
Mind of my Father.

Caroline Clancy

Sometimes nothing you say,
Is really understood.
Sometimes nothing you say,
Is even heard.
Sometimes you wonder why,
You actually speak at all.
Words that have so much meaning,
For one person,
Sometimes are meaningless to,
Others.
Frustrations caused,
Are utterly pointless when,
No one understands you at all.

My mind exists in the darkness of depression,
Caused by the many problems of late,
That I am overwhelmed at the number.
Nothing is as certain as the darkest depression.
It cuts out every last flicker of light from my life.
I didn't choose to be this way, I was doing okay.
Until that is, the discovery of my negligent,
Doctor, who turned me into a drug addict.
Sixteen months of withdrawals with,
No light showing at the end of the tunnel.
My body is screaming in protest, my mind in,
Darkness, so much so, I truly doubt,
I'm going to get out of this tunnel alive.
Truth is I'm beginning not to care,
The whole withdrawal process is taking too
long.
My stamina's gone, too long in the darkness,
Far, far too long indeed.

Broken Japanese jars,
Mended with gold.
Broken things made,
Beautiful once again.
Broken people, shattered,
Damaged, that's different.
Covering or filling or rebuilding,
The cracks that appear,
In our lives, our beings,
Is ultimately the best that we can do.
We can never be as we were before,
Aiming instead for a,
Better version of ourselves,
As we rebuild our lives,
Sometimes it works,
Other times it doesn't.
The idea is to keep on trying,
To put ourselves back together,
In a way that we can,
Live with thereafter.

I was never a child, not really,
In the sense that most people,
Understand children to be.
I was never a teenager either,
In the sense that people,
Understand teenagers to be.
Adulthood followed the,
Exact same pattern.
It's impossible to spend fifteen,
Years in Institutions,
And then find others too relate to.
All our lives are unique.
Mines just difficult for even,
Myself too relate to.
Thus I keep myself to myself,
For its difficult to socialise,
With married couples with,
Successful careers, homes,
And ordinary lives.
What do you do, they ask?
Where were you born?
Did you get along with your parents?
Well now, there's a story, I think.
Far far too complicated for me to explain.
I learned early most people don't,
Want the truth,
They want instead something,
They can relate too.
Life passes by,
From the moment,
Stretching backwards,
Stretching forwards.
Past, Present and Future.

I was an adult.
That became stuck in my,
Childhood.
It's impossible to move forwards,
Until the Padt has been,
Understood.
For without understanding,
There was only shame,
Self-hatred and self-blame.
Avoiding the issues of the Past,
Does nothing other than sustain the,
Past Suffering.
Insight is needed,
Validation of suffering.
Understanding of what happened,
And why,
In order to reorder,
Perspectives.
To be able to live in the Present,
To look to the Future,
Become someone without,
Self-hatred, blame and shame.

Pointing our finger at the Past
Blaming others for all our life's problems,
Doesn't help us at the end of the day.
Instead it stokes the fire of,
Injustices within our souls,
Spilling venomous hatred, rage and fury,
Into our minds relentlessly.
Negative feelings, provoked, repeatedly,
Do not go away.
There comes a time when as an adult,
We have to take responsibility,
For our own lives, in order to move on.
To do this we need to accept all,
Those things that we cannot change.
Validation of these feelings, acceptance,
Then turning away from the Past.
Blame only fuels hatred, hatred fuels Illnesses.
The only way to move forward is to leave,
Our Pasts behind us, where they belong,
We are adults now, responsible,
For our own happiness.
Blame becomes pointless,
Preventing healing and,
Ultimately moving forward,
With our lives.

Shadows on my bedroom wall,
Trigger flashbacks,
Of childhood trauma experienced.
There are many things in life,
That trigger memories of time Past.
Some surprising, some not,
That remind us of times we'd,
Rather forget.
But triggers often have no warnings,
Can occur in the strangest of circumstances,
Over the littlest things you'd never think of.
Like children's crayons, that sharp waxy smell.
My first instinct was to gag, wanting to vomit.
Reminders of childhood,
The pungent smell of plasticine had the,
Exact same effect,
As did the smell of warm creamy milk.
Triggered without warning.
These things and more,
Still occurring forty odd years after,
The traumatic experiences of my,
Own childhood.

I lived my whole childhood,
In a bubble of my own making.
Isolated and lonely,
With no one to talk too.
Real life was painful.
The adult world far too scary,
Living in a world like this.
Inside my body.
Inside my head.
Inside my mind.
No outlets, just isolation.
Loneliness creeping,
Like poisonous venom.
Into my veins, my body,
My mind.
Excruciating trauma,
Breaking my heart.
No one to talk to.
To witness.
To understand.
The breaking of a,
Child.

'Ring a ring of Roses,
Atishoo , Atishoo ,
We all fall down'.
Then it was the Black Plague.
In the 21st Century,
It's mental illness,
Suicide statistics,
Stigma. [45]

---

[45] This Nursery Rhyme was all about deaths from the Black Plague, a modern day equivalent could be called stigma and suicide rates surrounding mental illnesses.

My life lived in isolation,
Inside my body and in my mind.
Understanding as a young child,
That this wasn't 'normal'.
Silence and submission,
Secrets and Lies.
Isolating me repeatedly.
Cold ice inside my veins.
I forgot how to feel anything,
My mind became,
Distance and unreachable,
Even within myself.
Cold adult world rejection,
Outcast and abandoned,
Mentally, physically, emotionally,
Disappearing inside the silence,
Within myself.
Whilst my mind screamed,
Relentlessly.
Isolation cruel,
Lonely and cold,
Dissociating,
Distancing me,
Until finally,
I was unreachable,
To one and all,
Including my own self.

Death came to her,
Unbidden this time.
Without an invitation,
Nor a time or place.
Death told her,
Physically your body,
Is dying from inside,
To outside.
Poisonous addiction,
Murdering your mind.
I looked up at Death.
First time surprised.
I'd always gone to Death,
He'd never come for me.
Is it my time, I asked.
Soon, Death said unto me,
Sooner than you think.
Sooner than I thought.
Relief washed over me.
Finally,
I might Rest In Peace.

Bipolar disorder dissecting my mind,
Overwhelming overthinking,
Confusing absolutely everything.
Simple things becoming overreacting issues.
Over sensitivity making tears too easy.
Frustration sounding aggressive,
Instead of normal irritation.
Misunderstandings created thus,
Grappling with too much information,
Processed far too fast.
Moods a rollercoaster moving even faster.
Been stuck in the abyss of a dip,
Far too long now.
Major depressive disorder,
Wining and killing,
Destroying me once more.

Darkness was invisible to my eyes,
A monster within my mind.
A figment of horrific imagination,
A tentacled monster suffocating my body,
Of both oxygen and my life.
That I named it Darkness,
Was because as a young child,
I failed to understand,
That the only real monsters,
We're of the human kind.
Since Darkness always,
Arrived and left under,
The thick blanket of night.
Darkness at its darkest,
A monster that never spoke a single,
Human word,
As a child Darkness,
Traumatised my entire being.
A real monster living inside my head,
Inside my mind.

Sometimes if you look close enough,
You might notice a rare kind of beauty.
Amongst those damaged, broken, shattered,
By life experiences.
I've seen it myself before.
The quality of beauty that comes from,
Damaged people, it's in their understanding,
Often without any words to others.
A recognition of suffering.
These souls are older than they should be.
They recognise suffering in others instinctively.
Compassion, empathy and understanding,
Their ability to hear what your heart says.
Rare beauty from deep within.
As if you've met such a soul somewhere before,
Souls that have suffered,
Are often those that give most.
Relatable souls are beautiful, a rare,
Beauty born out of pain,
Someone that understands with kindness,
Compassion, empathy and love.

My Father, the authoritarian control freak,
Had a mind like no other,
I couldn't claim that I ever understood him.
I had no idea how he thought,
How his mind worked.
It was utterly beyond my comprehension,
As a child, a teenager, and as an adult.
He was highly intelligent, a perfectionist,
Without a doubt, but as for the way he thought
The complex intricacies of his thinking,
I never had 4he slightest clue.
How does a man such as he abuse,
His eldest daughter.
That his thinking was complex, irrational,
Bizarre, contorted and twisted,
Goes without saying.
He was impossible for me to understand,
To relate to at any age.
Whether it be as a child, or as an adult m
The workings of my Fathers mind,
Always remained an utter mystery to me.

Soul explosion,
Expelling the shame and dirt,
From inside.
Imploding mind,
Exploding misery mercifully.
Detonating the beginnings,
Of recovery.
Where memories of trauma,
Become less haunting.
Remembering less painful,
Forgiveness easier,
Forgetting impossible.
For the Past in remembering,
In talking, in understanding,
Becomes less controlling,
Moving on easier,
In the Living.

There was once a feeling,
That the insane were unclean.
Harbouring demons and dirt,
Within their minds.
They were treated with scorn,
Violence in the form of punishment,
Soul destroying tortuous behaviours,
Prisoners with absolutely no human rights.
There was no compassion,
For those affected by mental illness.
No empathy or understanding.

For they frightened the 'normal',
With hysterical behaviours,
Melancholic minds and misery.
Psychiatry then non-existent, the mind,
Not yet studied, long before,
Freud and John Locke.
Mental illnesses not understood,
Blatant shame and blame,
Relentless stigma rife.
Some things have changed since,
Others not as much as they should have done.

Death stalks the Shadowlands,
Walking with a certain attitude.
Knowing he'll get lucky each and every day,
For it's the one certainty of the living,
That they will in the die.
Death will come for each and everyone of us,
He only needs to bide his time,
Death is as patient as stoic.
Stalking the Shadowlands with the,
Clear knowledge that he will not n time find us.
That he is watching and waiting,
Patiently for our time to come.
Yet sometimes he is met by others,
Deliberately seeking escape from a,
Life of utter misery and madness.
Those are the suicides that,
Die before their time.
Death meets all that die with the same,
Deliberation and delivery of words,
From the Shadowlands of Life.

Gone girl faded with the passing of time,
Childhood memories and nightmares,
Lost in the early years,
Rediscovered during the adult years,
In order that gone girl may be laid to rest,
Back where she belongs,
In those traumatising childhood years.
For with the passing of the years,
Gone girl because petrified of moving on,
Not understanding where she should go.
Flashbacks and understanding,
Validation and forgiveness,
Freed her to move forward as the adult,
She'd already become.
Forgiving but not forgetting,
That for which she'd suffered with,
Years beyond her childhood,
Now laid to rest.

My Father stole my Innocence,
Violating both my body and my soul.
After which he brainwashed me,
With a relentless litany of lies.
Submissive and silent he,
Imprisoned my heart and mind,
Inside his own under lock and key.
Everything that was mine, was now his.
No boundaries, no self-identity
Nothing left that resembled me at all.
And years later no memories,
Of myself before.

Today I feel lost from myself,
Weeks of this feeling has left me,
Wondering whether I will ever,
Find myself again.
Those things that I loved,
Are no longer of interest to me.
Finding the will to do,
Anything,
Seems utterly impossible to me.
It's been so long since I was,
Happy, or even smiled.
It's exhausting even,
To pretend anymore.
I hate this feeling of,
Dissociating.
I've forgotten how to,
Move on.
I feel so lost from myself,
I can't pretend that,
I'm not, not to anyone.
Not anymore.

I thought of a Darkness as a monster,
For Darkness never spoke a word.
Merely made scary sounds.
It was three decades before I understood,
The reality of Darkness's identity.
Childhood trauma returned,
In flashbacks that told the truth.
There was no monster,
Other than my Father.
But as a child in the darkness of night,
I believed I was visited by,
A real monster of the night.
I dreamt of this monster relentlessly,
As a child in my nightmares.
In these terrible dreams,
The monster bore no resemblance,
To any human of any kind.
Now o& course I understand,
That the only real monsters,
Are indeed of the human kind.

A child born without any roots,
Unloved and Outcast,
Becomes stuck firmly in Time.
For a child such as this grows,
Her own roots.
The trouble is that these roots,
Are contorted and twisted,
Unhealthy and dead.
It's not the child's fault,
But those that do not care,
That do not love and nurture her,
Those are the ones at fault, not her.
Instead there was rejection and trauma,
These terrifying experiences,
Created a bizarre way of thinking.
No one tells the child any different.
So the whole of this child's identity,
Is rooted in secrets and lies.
Thus without knowing,
She grows with no understanding,
Believing that she is at fault,
For that's the way she's,
Been brought up.

The unlovable traumatised child,
Eventually grew into a teenager.
Her childhood had been traumatic,
The teenage years were worse,
For different reasons,
Reasons she couldn't possibly understand,
Since she'd suffered,
Traumatic amnesia at the age of eight,
Leaving her with no memory,
Of those first eight childhood years.
Had she remembered,
Then her teenage years may have been,
Far less confusing, but this wasn't the case,
So her Fathers words seemed,
Utterly bizarre when he called her,
His wench, a slut, a whore,
His Scarlet woman, his busty blonde.
Words that disgusted her.
Body shaming and mockery.
She thought it obvious,
That she'd never been with any man,
Was absolutely terrified of hands and touch.
That her Father should call her these names,
She simply couldn't understand.
Her Father seemed oblivious,
To the absolute obvious.
She failed to understand him at all.
Her clothes were conservative,(cont..)

Make-up she never once wore.
She felt utterly ashamed and utterly,
Clueless as to why her Father treated,
And talked to her like this.
Clueless and oblivious to her earlier years,
She suffered repeatedly,
From shame and humiliation,
Absolutely confused,
Remaining this way for years to come.
Until the flashbacks started.

By the time she was eighteen years old,
She was a complete and utter mess.
No self-identity, no confidence,
And no self-esteem feeling worthless.
And her Father continued to push her,
From pillar to post, to different Universities.
Since she had no ideas of her own,
No idea what she wanted to do with her life.
By this time she was exceedingly aware that,
From the age of eight years old,
There was something seriously wrong with her.
For nowhere did she fit in, rejected,
And bullied constantly at home, at school.
By eighteen she finally understood,
That this was going to end very very badly,
Though she still didn't know how.
She despised herself utterly,
Was terrified of people, and living in her head,
Absolutely scared of everything.
Not knowing what to do with herself.
Least of all what to do with her life,
Least of all that.

After my Degree the speed,
Of my determination accelerated.
An exponential increase in self-harm,
Due to feeling lost and confused.
So terrified of the way I was feeling,
With absolutely no understanding of why,
I was such an utter mess within.
It felt as if I were continually sliding,
At high speed down a deep dark hole,
At an ever increasing speed,
In ever decreasing circles.
Believing myself utterly insane,
Without anyone to talk too,
I found I couldn't stop myself falling,
Falling, falling, towards,
Self-destruction,
Even had I wanted to for I was,
Running at full pelt,
Downhill faster and faster.
Towards my end. [46]

---

[46] I achieved a 1st Class degree in Education, Philosophy, Theology and Ethics. I taught for a year. Then I began an MA degree during the course of which I had my breakdown and ended up being abandoned in the Asylum

Then came the fateful day when,
Fire and Ice,
Met in the middle and crashed.
I collapsed.
My body protesting,
It no longer wanted to pretend,
That I was alright.
Truth be told I'd been expecting,
This very moment for a lifetime,
Momentarily, I felt relieved,
Not to have to pretend to others,
That I could keep on going.
Instead there was something very wrong,
At the very least I was insane.
What I hadn't expected,
And perhaps should have,
Was the immediate rejection,
By every last member of my family.
Total abandonment followed,
By one and all.

Abandoned in the Asylum,
None of them looked back once.
The shock wave that struck me,
Was as strong as a tsunami,
As violent as a thunderstorm could be.
Absolute total abandonment.
The abandonment issues that followed,
Were utterly appalling,
Lasting decades afterwards.
For I finally understood just how,
Completely I was unloved.
With this mass abandonment,
Went every last tiny she'd of hope.
Left, I willingly slid to,
The very bottom of,
The Abyss.

She learned more the day she,
Was abandoned,
Her first day in the Asylum.
Than she'd learned in her lifetime,
Right up to that very moment.
For she finally understood exactly,
How unloved she actually was.
Up until that same moment,
She'd lived in hope,
That she might have been wrong.
That they might have loved her after all.
She'd been wrong.
For they never phoned her,
Visited or wrote a card,
Or tried to talk to her at all.
Instead from that exact moment,
She was outcast and dead to them.
They couldn't bear the stigma and shame,
Of having a daughter in the 'nut house',
They couldn't bear her at all.
Not a single family member,
Or a relative of hers ever spoke to her,
For the following fifteen years.
She was entirely alone,
Abandoned completely by those that,
She'd called Family.

She wanted to crawl into,
The deepest darkest hole,
The shame she felt at being abandoned,
By every member of her entire family,
Was too much it broke her heart,
Shattered illusions of being saved,
By her own family,
Was on many occasions nearly,
The death of her.
All she wanted was to hide away,
Be more invisible than ever before.
She was worse than worthless,
She was absolutely nothing at all,
Nothing at all,
But mad, sad and very bad.

Trauma leaves a permanent stamp,
On ones body and mind.
A stamp so powerful it cannot,
Ever be entirely erased.
Showing itself in a medley,
Of different ways.
Hyper-Vigilance,
Body awareness and difficulty
Trusting others.
Relationship problems,
The 'startle' reflex,
Dissociative behaviour,
Overthinking and depression.
Physically the body remembers so much,
Psychological reactions,
To traumatic experiences,
Of such that the body,
Never forgets.

She wasn't long in the Asylum,
Before every single ounce of her,
Began to unravel.
It was as if the stitches,
That had held her together,
Were no more than of,
Finest Cotton.
There had been almost,
Nothing holding,
Her together for years.
Pandora's box sprang open,
Spinning her into the Abyss,
Utterly terrifying her,
Fully understanding that,
She'd never be able to hold herself,
Together as she had done so before and,
The chances of resealing Pandora's box,
We're now nigh impossible.
All that her Father had hated,
Her family turned their backs on,
Every single fault of hers,
Would to her utter shame,
Be displayed for all to see.

Her entire Life had been consumed in silence,
Every feeling she'd ever felt for as long,
As she could remember had been invalidated.
Now she'd lost the art of self-expression.
Years of submissive obedience had,
Finally taken their toll.
They wanted her to talk about her feelings,
Yet she couldn't identify any feelings.
She'd become used to saying 'I'm fine',
As a teenager, and then as an adult.
She'd lost connection with her feelings,
A lifetime ago, she hadn't any feelings,
As far as she was concerned.
She wasn't even aware of the empty,
Void within her body and soul.
Asked to define anger, she hadn't a clue.
Same for every other feeling,
That they asked her to describe.
So she tried to make them tell her the ,
Right answer, if second guess them,
Terrified as she was of giving,
The wrong answer.
She had no idea how to fill,
The all consuming silence that had,
Blanketed her for so many years,
No idea at all.
Unaware then that she'd have to,
Learn to feel all over again.
As a Child,
Every feeling I expressed,
Was denied,
Invalidated.
As a child,

Every word I spoke,
Was denied,.
Invalidated.
As a child,
Every negative experience,
Was denied,
Invalidated.
Nothing in my life,
Was ever,
Validated.
As a child,
I was denied,
Invalidated,
Confused.
My life was worthless,
To those that mattered to me.
Leaving me confused and terrified,
Of my mind and my feelings,
Which were always so very wrong.

My Father was a charismatic man,
University graduate twice over.
All that knew him,
Respected him.
My Father was that kind of man,
A wife, three children,
Two daughters and the long,
Awaited Son.
Everything he turned his hand to,
He perfected.
He wanted me to follow,
In his footsteps,
To be perfect.
That I failed to live up to,
My Fathers standards,
Was a cause of much derision.
I was the hyper-sensitive child,
The one he punished,
For not being good enough.
I tried so very hard to please him.
But he'd by then selected me as his target.
The failure, to vent his frustrations upon.
In truth, I never stood a chance,
He understood this too.
For it was I that was his problem.

As a child,
I found by default,
A coping skill,
That must have been instinctive.
When Darkness arrived late at night,
I remember being terrified of dying.
Terrified of choking to death,
Of suffocation.
My body and soul split.
My soul would fly up to the ceiling above.
Whereupon I'd turn and look down.
I'd see my body from high up,
Watch what Darkness was doing to my body,
With absolutely no feelings.
When Darkness left,
I'd feel myself sucked back down,
Inside my body.
It was over two decades later,
Before I heard the term,
Dissociation.
Understood it for what it was,
A coping skill that,
Protected my Soul.

When I was eight years old,
My paternal grandfather died.
A sudden heart attack they said.
The trauma of that day has never,
Gone away.
I sensed my grandfathers death,
Before my Father himself knew.
I didn't understand how I'd known,
I just knew.
When my Father told me that his,
Father had died,
I was utterly terrified that my sensing,
My grandfathers death,
Had actually caused him to die,
My thoughts had killed him.
I believed I'd murdered him,
By thinking thoughts,
I couldn't have known.
I was terrified my Father would discover,
What I'd done, I couldn't tell him.
For some reason the sexual abuse,
Stopped at this time.
Most likely due to the double trauma,
I then developed traumatic amnesia,
Forgetting entirely,
My first eight years of life.
This amnesia stayed with me for,
The next two decades and more.(cont..)

It was only after my own fathers death,
Whilst I'd already been,
In the Asylum two years,
That the flashbacks started, [47]
Of my life before the age of eight.

---

[47] Self harm was something I resorted to at the age of 19 years. I only found it helpful for reliving internal stress for less than a year. Following that I used other coping skills. Thirty years on and my scars are barely visible.

Self-harm,
To keep calm.
Pent up.
Bottled,
Feelings.
Pressure cooker,
Inside my head.
Worthless,
No one hears,
Or wants to listen.
Head exploding,
Self-hatred,
Overflowing.
Fuels,
Self-harm,
Cut my arm,
Crimson blood,
Dripping,
From my fingers,
Release,
Relief.
Calming down.
Truth,
About,
Self-harm.

Don't believe everything you're told.
Believe in your gut feelings,
Before anything else.
Over the decade in the Asylum,
I was given over fifteen different diagnoses.
I chose not to believe everything I was told.
They seemed to desperate to,
Label me with one diagnoses or another.
One after er another, and I lost all,
Faith in the Consultants ability,
To diagnose me correct for he was always,
Changing his mind, and the medication.
I grew tired of all the different,
Psychiatric labels.
I decided in the end,
That the best diagnosis was the one,
I made up myself,
'Messed-up woman'.
As far as I could see it covered,
Every possibility without categorising me.
This was the only diagnoses I ,
Settled for in the decade,
Locked up in the Asylum of old.

Death,
Excruciating.
Tortuous,
Pain,
Terrifying,
Terrorising,
End of Life,
And Living.
Death.
Loss of hearing,
Due to screaming.
Blood vessels pumping.
Rain freezing.
Chest heaving.
Hardly breathing.
Gasping.
Convulsing.
Blinding,
Pain.
Death is not pretty,
Remember this.
Death.
Ending.
Buried.
Rotting.
Decaying.
Forgotten.
Lost in Time.

These eyes of mine have,
Seen far too much.
Mine is the face that has,
Suffered too much.
These ears of mine have,
Heard too much.
This body of mine has,
Felt too much.
I saw too much.
I suffered too much.
I heard too much,
I felt too much.
But,
I Survived.

Recovery is hard,
Without a single doubt. [48]
But it is worth it,
To gain a life worth living.
It won't be the same life you once had,
Before the trauma, the mental illness.
It will be different, but better than,
The suffering you've been through.
Never ever give up trying,
I know how very hard it is I've been there.
If, like I, you fall down, relapse,
Get straight back up again, move on.
However many times you fall,
I fell many a time,
Always pick yourself up and try again.
Stand tall, you can do this,
With commitment and self-belief.
Every single time you fall,
Remember why you started,
This journey of Recovery.
Never ever give up on your life,
You're worth far more than you think.
Every single one of us is unique,
We all deserve a better Life,
No exceptions, none at all.

---

[48] Mental illnesses should never be glamourised. The suffering is real. No one would choose to have a mental illness of any kind. There are far better more enjoyable choices in life, no one chooses to suffer in this way.

I feel sunlight on my face,
It lights me up inside.
Bringing relief from the darkness,
I always saw in my earlier life.
At the bottom of the Abyss,
No light ever shined.
Clawing me way out of the abyss,
I slipped and slid on the way up,
Digging my feet in hard.
Fingernails refusing to give,
I crawled over the rim,
To feel the blessed sun on my face,
I'd once forgotten, rediscovered.
It was twenty years before,
I fell that far again.
The climb took time,
But was worth it.
The lightness of being,
Myself at last.

I suffered mutism, [49]
Several times over two decades.
The longest period of mutism,
Lasted three years long.
The shortest about six months.
Trauma stole my voice,
Making my silent.
Unable to speak, to say a word,
Reduced to communication,
With pen and paper.
Some patients assumed I was deaf,
Or blind, others an imbecile,
Who would shout directly into my face.
As if I were a strange alien,
From outer space.
Some outcast who had her,
Tongue cut out.
A weird woman who writes,
Communicates with pen and paper.
Certainly not 'normal',
Definitely abnormal.
I got used to these reactions,
And they got used to me.

---

[49] Mutism was a condition I suffered from on more than a few occasions. The first bout of mutism occurred after a traumatic experience without any warning. After this I suffered long periods of Elective Mutism, probably due to the fact I felt "unheard", which in the Asylum was terribly frustrating. Later a suffered my longest period of mutism that lasted from beginning to end almost 3years.

Stranded on the edge of Life,
Walking the narrow tightrope,
Between the living and the dead.
I'd wonder what the point was,
Living hat is.
A single straight line,
Between the Living,
And the Dead.
It took years of my life,
To choose which side of this line,
I wanted to be,
Stranded on the edge of Life,
For years I failed to,
Understand the difference,
Of being either,
Dead or Alive.
Both felt the same to me.
No distinction no decision.
Which was the better side?
Living or dead.
I really didn't understand.
Took years to choose,
Life.

Touch,
I hated it.
I hated being touched.
Sexually abused.
I hated being touched.
Physically abused.
I hated being touched.
Assaulted by a stranger.
I hated being touched.
Raped at thirty,
I hated being touched.
A sexually abused child,
Not taught boundaries,
Believed her body,
Belonged to others.
Not to her.
Her body wasn't hers.
Adolescence and Adulthood,
Proved this repeatedly.
Touch.
Painful.
Choking.
Terrifying.
Terrorising.
Hands that touch.
Hurting, hurting, hurting.
Powerlessness.
Touch hurts, avoid touch.
X
Darkness watched over me,
Like a huge Raven,
Throughout my entire childhood.
It's wings were wide and strong,

Stretched right over me.
It's claws were sharp,
Too tight, to wriggle free.
Darkness accompanied,
My life, my nightmares,
My childhood years.
It's heart was stronger,
It's beak brought untold pain.
Darkness engulfed me.
Tore the life from me.
Traumatised and terrified me.
Haunted my nightmares.
Ostracised me until the end,
Of its life, and then some more.
The wings of Darkness,
Blocked out years of light.
Darkness itself in all its strength,
Never quite left,
Some small parts remain,
Lodged deep inside my mind.
Like sharp pieces of shrapnel,
From a war long passed,
But never quite forgotten.
X
The black dog of depression,
Causing misery and suffering.
Like black storm clouds,
Invading minds and destroying,
Lives.
The key to depression,
Is in our own minds related to our,
Internal ability to change.
Day by day taking small steps,

Away from the Black Dog,
Towards a better frame of mind.
Again the only person to make,
These deliberate small changes,
Lies within us our individual,
Responsibility.
Without the will to change,
Nothing can be done,
The only person that can save us,
Is ourselves,
We cannot be saved by anyone else.
So changing our mindset,
As difficult as it can be, is the only answer,
To recovering from depression.
Positive thoughts replacing negativity,
The answer to beating off,
The black dog of depression.

I was sexually abused,
Early in my childhood life.
Darkness came to visit,
On the darkest of darkest nights.
Terrifying and traumatising,
Almost killing me.
My body frozen in fear.
As Darkness forced itself,
Inside my mouth.
Fear of suffocating,
Unable to breathe,
Dissociating.
Imminent death.
Heart racing,
Lungs straining,
Mouth full.
Dying.
Traumatised.
Repeatedly by Darkness,
The fear of suffocating,
Terrifying.
I was a sexually abused, [50]
Child.

---

[50] Oral sexual abuse

My Father destroyed my childhood.
The effects and the consequences,
Of childhood sexual and physical abuse,
Have lasted my entire life.
You destroy a child,
You destroy a teenager,
You destroy the adult too.
Childhood trauma,
Complex post traumatic stress disorder.
Terrifying and destructive,
Sending seismic ripples throughout,
My entire life.
Moving forward always a struggle.
Leaving the Past where it belongs,
Moving on,
Forgiving but not forgetting,
That's how trauma works,
Hyper-vigilance.
Startle effect.
So many small things,
Connecting back.
Take a child's innocence,
You change its life,
Permanently.
Cause and effect,
Rippling through the years.
PTSD remaining,
Reminding all through ones life.
The Asylum,
Built in 1886, the Victorian era.
A monstrously ugly building,
Gothic architecture,
Grey stone cold,

Pollution grey.
Faded green Institutional,
Peeling, dirty walls.
Old linoleum cracked,
Stained carpets,
Frayed armchairs.
Outdated, uncomfortable.
Smells of unwashed bodies,
Blood, vomit, urine.
Over cooked institutional,
Sloppy food.
Two huge dormitories,
Mixed sex,
No privacy other than,
Torn curtains separating,
Each bed.
The Victorian Asylum,
An insane nightmare.

Anxiety,
My pulse is beating far too fast.
There are beads of sweat forming,
On my forehead.
My stomach queasy,
My hands trembling.
The crowded pavement,
Engulfing me.
My feet staggering,
Swept along in the tide of people.
Anxiety becoming overwhelming.
Panic starting,
Feelings of imminent death,
Heart beat thundering on my ear drums,
Pain rippling through my body,
Feeling as if I'm having a,
Heart attack.
Sinking to my knees,
Tears rolling down my cheeks,
Gasping for breath.
Breathe, breathe, breathe.
And then just as I'm sure I'm about to die,
My body slumps exhausted,
Running free of adrenaline,
Anxiety passes by,
Until the next time.

Run rabbit, run, run, run.
A cars a coming run rabbit run.
Paralysed by the headlights,
Frozen in the moment,
The rabbits choice is,
Flight or Fight.
I was like every young child,
Abused in their own home.
Too young too innocent to fight.
I failed to develop this skill early on.
Through no fault of my own.
Vulnerable because of this.
Men took advantage whenever,
They wished.
I couldn't run, nor could I fight.
Standing frozen instead.
Awaiting ,
The oncoming car wreck,
Blinded by panic.

Once locked in the Asylum.
Flight wasn't an option,
I learned to fight with words instead.
Battled the Consultant Psychiatrist,
The egotistical bastard,
With words, more words,
Debates, logic, well thought out,
Discussion and common sense,
Thinking out of the box.
We are not angels waiting to die,
Instead we are moral beings,
Hurting inside.
We are not angels waiting to die,
We are those needing help,
The ones that that are traumatised,
Upset, confused, depressed,
Deep within our minds.
We might say that we wish to die,
Indeed many of us do just that.
But the words we speak are due to lack of,
Compassion, empathy and understanding,
Care and love and help,
Are the things that we really want.
We are not angels waiting to die,
We are the hurting ones not knowing,
Which way to turn for,
The help we so badly need. (cont..)

Our minds are overflowing with pain,
What we need is help, don't you see?
To share the almighty burden,
That's weighing our body and souls down.
Someone to share the burden of our pain.
We are not angels waiting to die,
We're crying out for the,
Help we so desperately need.

Do not judge me harshly,
Until you've walked a mile with me.
In my shoes, my mind.
Try to understand with empathy,
Compassion and kindness.
My life, my trauma, my pain.
I did not choose this life I've led.
Traumatised as a child,
By my own Father, who owned me.
Abused my body, my mind, my soul.
In every imaginable way.
Violating my body, my trust.
Do not judge me harshly,
I've already suffered too much.
My Father stole my innocence,
Tortured my mind and my soul,
Leaving me in a million tiny pieces,
Broken, shattered, alone.
Do not judge me harshly,
I did not choose this life of mine.
Decades it took to mend myself,
Changing from Victim to Survivor.
Do not judge me harshly,
Reject me, ignore my life.,
For I am a Survivor,
I don't want your pity, or platitudes,
I want instead your time.
In a World so intolerant, (cont..)

To mental illnesses,
Turning away from those like I,
That have suffered mentally,
And worked hard to survive,
Be gentle, be kind,
Treat those who've suffered,
With the respect and understanding,
That they deserve.

Anguished pain residing,
Inside every part of my mind.
This mental pain that's so very acute,
Feels worse than most,
Physical pain I've felt.
Overwhelming even logical thought,
Mind alight with the throbbing,
Relentless pain of trauma.
Post traumatic stress disorder.
Childhood long past now,
Still remembered.
Painful thoughts screaming,
Repeatedly inside my own mind.
Wanting it to stop,
Tears streaming down my face,
Not enough to relieve,
The ferocity of this mind pain.
Self-harm helped for a while,
Red blood, the vivid colour of the pain.
Mind screaming for some peace,
Red seeping from my broken skin,
Short term solace,
Replaced eventually with different,
Less destructive coping skills.
Slowly the pain over time abated,
Turning into words and validation,

Always,
Be Yourself.
Don't Try To Mimic Others.
You Hold As,
Good Examples.
Instead,
Be Yourself,
And Be True To Yourself.
It's The Only Way,
To Live Your Life,
Truly,
Truthfully,
Respect,
Yourself.
Always.

How often have I felt trapped,
By the borders of mental illness.
How often have I felt constrained by a diagnosis.
That would cause me to settle for,
A life of extremes.
How often have I rejected a diagnosis,
Purely because of the feeling,
Of being locked into a definition,
A diagnostic criteria.
How often have I felt trapped,
By the symptoms of a diagnosis,
Unable to live as I've wanted instead,
Constrained by a psychiatric diagnosis.
Mindset is indeed all that it took,
To free myself,
From the definitions of diagnoses,
That threaten to overwhelm,
The living of my life.
In the end the only diagnosis,
Acceptable to me,
Is that of messed-up woman,
Which hasn't any constraints and definitions,
Like a psychiatric illness threatens.

Stigma,
Separating the suffering,
From the ignorant. [51]
Those that turn away,
Fearful of mental illness.
Those that walk away,
Without caring,
Afraid of mental illness,
As if it were contagious.
Those that are ignorant,
In the 21st Century,
Of mass technological,
Available information.
Are without a doubt,
Thoughtless cowards.

---

[51] The fact that ignorance makes up a large amount of the cause behind mental illness stigma is unacceptable in today's technological society, where information is free at the touch of a button.

Caroline Clancy

I live in Norwich. I am 51 years old and have two children. I have a degree in Education, Philosophy, Ethics and Theology, I was a Teacher. I am now disabled with fibromyalgia.

I started writing poetry to raise awareness of mental health issues and the related stigma surrounding this subject. I suffered an abusive childhood. As a young adult I had a 'breakdown ' and was admitted to an Asylum. I spent a decade locked up, before being moved to other Institutions. I am diagnosed with Complex PTSD, Bipolar Disorder, Anxiety Disorder, Depression. I struggled hard and made a Recovery before having my children. My poetry covers all issues from Childhood to the present day.

.

www.ingramcontent.com/pod-product-compliance
Lightning Source LLC
Chambersburg PA
CBHW031510270326
41930CB00006B/335